BAKING BY FEEL

recipes to sort out your emotions (whatever they are today!) with playful twists on classic cookies, cakes, pies, and more

Baking
by
Feel

Becca Rea-Tucker
@thesweetfeminist

PHOTOGRAPHY BY AMY SCOTT ~ FOOD STYLING BY OLIVIA CAMINITI

HARPER WAVE

An Imprint of HarperCollinsPublishers

HarperCollins books may be purchased for educational, business, or sales promotional use. For information, please email the Special Markets Department at SPsales@harpercollins.com.

FIRST EDITION

Designed by Leah Carlson-Stanisic

Food photography by Amy Scott; all other images courtesy of Shutterstock, Inc Shutterstock, Inc.

Library of Congress Cataloging-in-Publication Data has been applied for.

ISBN 978-0-06-316004-0

22 23 24 25 26   LSC   10 9 8 7 6 5 4 3 2 1

THIS BOOK IS DEDICATED TO MY SWEET AND KIND HUSBAND, RHYS.
THE NUMBER OF DISHES HE WASHED IN SERVICE OF THIS BOOK IS ASTOUNDING.

Contents

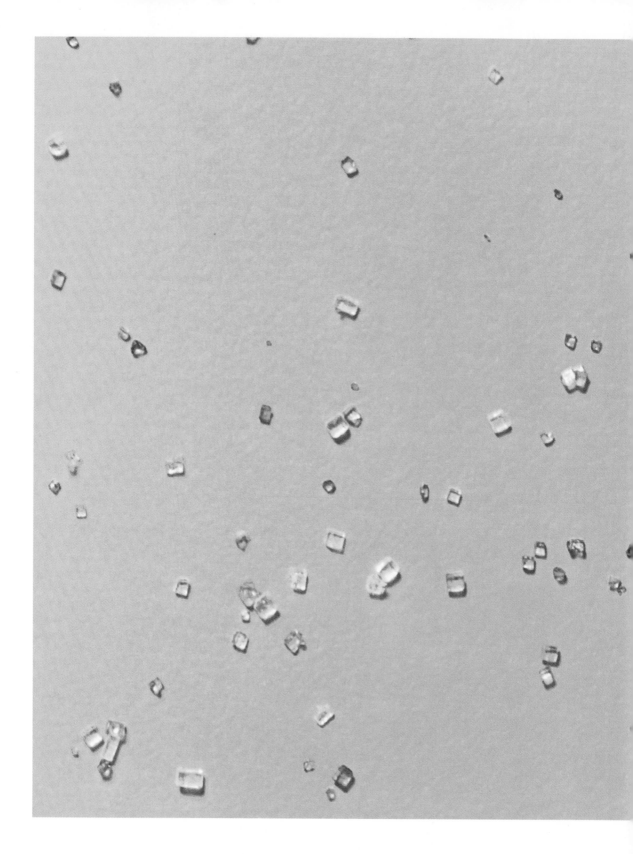

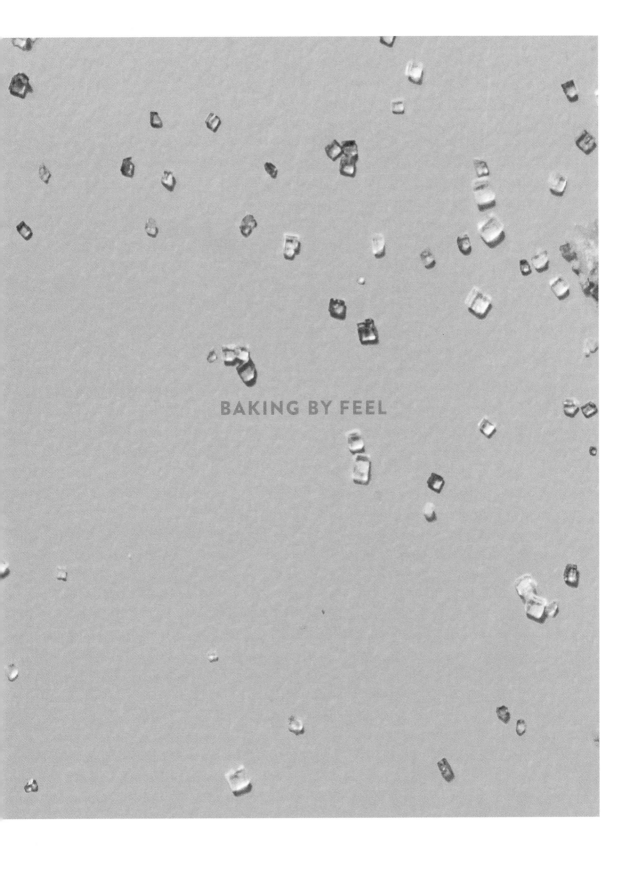

BAKING BY FEEL

introduction

In the process of writing this book, I spent a lot of time researching a variety of resources about exploring our emotions. In the process, I discovered that there are a *lot* of books written for children about understanding their emotions (special shout-out to Madalena Moniz's beautiful book *Today I Feel . . . An Alphabet of Feelings*). We recognize that an important part of a child's development is gaining the ability to identify, name, and understand emotions. As we get older—though our emotions grow in nuance and complexity—we seem to think we're done with this learning process. Yet, sometimes (quite often, really!) we grown-ups need some support to sort through our emotions too. Navigating the complex waters of our feelings is a lifelong process.

Of course, there are many books about feelings for adults as well, but in my experience the majority of them are focused on identifying emotions for the purpose of overcoming them or fixing them, rather than *feeling* them. With this framing, feelings become something to be handled rather than explored curiously. And if your goal is simply to "handle" your feelings, you can miss out on a ton of helpful stuff. Your feelings serve a multitude of purposes: to help you orient yourself in the world, to protect you, to guide you, and to connect you with other feeling-havers. Yes, they're messy, but so what? To be clear, I am not a psychologist, therapist, or social worker. I am simply a human with a few decades of lived experience feeling (and also *not* feeling) my feelings. And, of course, an experienced baker!

Remember those super cool Choose Your Own Adventure books you read as a kid? This book is like a grown-ups-who-like-baking version of that genre. If at this moment you're like, "What are you talking about, I've never heard of those," think of this book as an interactive resource with some more structure (and excitement!) than your standard cookbook. I've compiled a comprehensive list of feelings across the emotional spectrum and developed a recipe with each one in mind. Now here's where you come in: you can choose what to bake based on what you're feeling—whatever that is.

An important note: This book is emotionally agnostic. In other words: whatever you're feeling, it's 100 percent OK. I don't think it's very helpful to spend time sorting feelings into buckets of "good" or "bad," for a variety of reasons. When we label a feeling as "bad," we often wind up inadvertently shaming ourselves for experiencing it. When really, we have nothing to be ashamed of! And, if we spend a lot of time trying to ascertain whether a feeling is OK to experience, we might actually avoid feeling it.

I understand the impulse to avoid the "feeling" part of feelings, as someone who defaults to intellectualizing them. I can describe an emotion to you in perfect detail, like: the sharp embarrassment of losing the spelling bee in sixth grade by misspelling the word *escalator* in front of an auditorium full of people; the stinging heartache when someone who I thought was the love of my life (but turned out to just be my college boyfriend) suddenly broke up with me over FaceTime; or the fuzzy pride that came from relearning how to ride a bike at twenty-nine. But it's much harder for me to fully experience those feelings. In fact, for the vast majority of my years earthside I didn't even know there was a difference between understanding and feeling. But once my (brilliant, wonderful) therapist gently pointed out the distinction, I set out to try to *feel*. That's way easier said than done, of course, but I've found that it's more possible for me to experience and process my feelings while I'm working with my hands. So, I do lots of creative things when I feel an emotion coming on. I knit, I make pasta, I garden, I make vision boards, and most of all, I bake.

In my grandma's house in Wichita, Kansas, there was always something homemade and sweet to snack on: chocolate chip cookies, ice cream cake, butterscotch pie. I grew up watching her bake. As a teenager, I started baking my own cakes from boxed mixes. As I grew more confident, I left the boxes behind and started baking from scratch, eventually developing my own recipes. I bake when I'm happy, when I have a bad day, when I'm looking for answers, and of course when it's someone's birthday.

It's common for people to use cooking and baking as an emotional outlet. During the COVID-19 pandemic, there was a widely publicized groundswell of interest in baking (remember the sourdough phase?), with cookbook and all-purpose flour sales spiking for months. Confined to their homes during

a time of existential threat, a lot of people turned to baking for its therapeutic value. Baking can help us cope, and this book is designed to support you in that effort as you bake through all your feels.

I like to think of my recipes as approachable and a touch nostalgic. They are for the kinds of treats that your grandmother might have made, updated with some modern techniques, flavors, and twists. They are unfussy and flavor-focused. I'm also a self-taught baker, so I totally get the need for clear instructions that incorporate sensory cues, like "work the butter into the flour mixture with your fingertips until the largest pieces are the size of black beans"! In this book, I will encourage you to trust yourself and bake by sight, smell, taste, and emotion. I'm talking *literally* baking by feel.

For the past few years, I've been "saying it with sugar" by decorating cakes with feminist (defined broadly!) messages and posting them on the internet as The Sweet Feminist.

I hit upon a variety of topics—from voting rights, to street harassment, to abortion access. In the beginning, it was an anonymous project. As I grew more confident in my voice, I added my name to it. Over time, I became more and more visible in my work: vulnerabilities, dreams, wins, and losses. It's an honest reflection of my own life, both the sweet and salty! When I started the project, I knew that I'd be sharing my voice with others. What I didn't expect was how many people would share their voices with me! Through my work as The Sweet Feminist, people have offered up their joys, pains, worries, and experiences. I'm continually in awe of the abundance of genuine and authentic humans who exist in the world, and their willingness to connect over shared (or sometimes differing!) experiences. Also, the near universal love of cake.

I decided to write *Baking by Feel* because it was what I needed. But I wrote it as if I were talking (and offering some gentle advice) to my best friend. It's based on the firm belief that you are wonderful and worthy of care in all of your emotional realities and moods. Your complexity deserves to be seen and appreciated! I hope this book helps you celebrate your joys, untangle your big and small challenges, and see yourself more clearly. I also hope it helps you learn how to whip up a batch of Swiss buttercream so easily you'll be pretty sure you could do it with your eyes closed.

This book is for you, whatever you're feeling today.

Chapter 1

how to use this book

an abbreviated list of the therapeutic benefits of baking

We'll talk about these in (a lot) more depth throughout the book, but to start:

It puts you in touch with your senses! Imagine:

* The way pie crust feels when you work in the butter with your fingertips.
* The way powdered sugar kisses your cheeks when you make frosting.
* The way the cake smells when it's done (that warm nuttiness!).
* The way the egg white slips through your fingers when you're separating it from the yolk.

Working with your hands grounds you in the present moment. You might:

* Temporarily forget about that huge project that's due next week because you're in the zone, rolling cookie dough into perfectly round spheres that are exactly the same weight down to the gram. (Yes, I weigh out my cookies by the gram.)

It helps you connect with people you love (or just like) by literally nourishing them. Such as when:

* Your neighbor is sick, so you bring them a giant batch of cookies.
* Your best friend gets a promotion, so you whip up her fave chocolate pie.

* You family is able to gather in person on Christmas Eve, so you bring snowball cookies.

Speaking of nourishment, it also gives you an opportunity to nourish yourself!

* Make *your* favorite recipe, without worrying if it's what someone else will like.
* Like other creative pursuits, baking can help interrupt cyclical thoughts or self-criticism.
* Working through a complex recipe (say, my Coffee-Glazed Cinnamon Rolls [page 81]) will force you to focus in on something other than your own (perhaps unhelpful) thoughts.

Trying something new/learning a new skill lends a feeling of accomplishment. Maybe you:

* Make a layer cake from scratch when you're usually more of a boxed mix type of person.
* Brown butter without burning the shit out of it.
* Assess at a glance when the butter and sugar are *actually* creamed together.

There's a lot of pleasure in the sensory work of baking: scrumptious tastes, mouth-watering smells, and satisfying tactile sensations. Take pleasure in:

* Smashing graham crackers into tiny pieces for your graham cracker pie crust.

* Breathing in the smell of cinnamon wafting through your home.
* Snacking on that leftover bit of cookie dough.

Organizing your mise en place can help organize your mind. Yes, really (see page 16).

* Measure out all your ingredients before you even turn on your oven.
* Lay them out in the order you'll need them.
* Pull out all the tools you'll need: bowls, measuring cups and spoons, spatula, whisk, cake pan. And don't forget the oven mitts!

wait, how do I use this book?

Excellent question, I'm so glad you asked! There are a few options:

THE "TRADITIONAL COOKBOOK" WAY

You use this book like a normal cookbook. Just flip through and make whatever strikes your fancy, feelings aside. A bit boring, but you do you!

THE "FOLLOW YOUR FEELINGS" WAY (ALSO KNOWN AS THE EXCITING WAY)

First, reference the emotions wheel (see page 8) to identify what you're feeling today. And remember, it doesn't have to be just one thing! Often, we're feeling a whole mix of emotions at once.

After you've identified the feelings that come to the surface, peruse the recipe pairings and determine what you'd like to make and/or which emotion you'd most like to explore today.

While you're baking up a storm, take a few minutes to read about the emotion and work on any accompanying exercises. The goal is to use the act of baking as a sensory experience to help you feel and process your feelings. The bonus is a sweet treat to share with people you love. Or enjoy hot from the oven, by yourself, standing up!

Now, this method does take some trust, both because it requires you to slow down and look inward *and* because it requires you to let someone else (me!) choose what you're making. But it's what this book was made for, baby, so give it a shot!

THE "I JUST WANT COOKIES" WAY

You've felt your feelings, you promise. You've done the exercises, journaled your heart out, and consulted the emotions wheel. You're just here to remake your fave cookie recipe for that potluck you're going to tomorrow. This is very much allowed!

identifying & naming emotions

ROBERT PLUTCHIK'S EMOTIONS WHEEL

Psychologist Robert Plutchik first proposed the emotions wheel in the 1980s as a way to illustrate the range of human emotions. Plutchik's wheel—a part of his larger theory of emotion—is made up of eight primary emotions grouped into opposites: joy and sadness, fear and anger, anticipation and surprise, and trust and disgust. He proposed

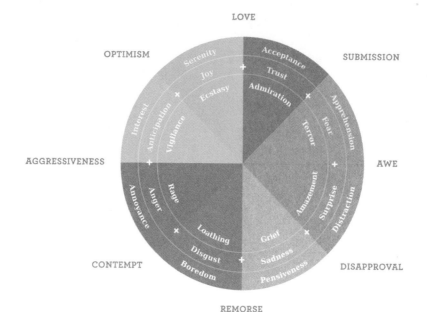

that these core emotions are the building blocks for all of the others. Plutchik's wheel also visualized the idea that emotions vary in intensity. As you move toward the outside of the wheel, the emotions intensify in complexity, quality, and color.

When I worked as an assistant at a preschool in college, one of my very favorite activities was when a child would call me over to our school's version of this wheel—a simpler emotions chart that could be easily understood by toddlers—to discuss their (often big!) feelings. In case you haven't visited a preschool recently, I'm describing a poster with a variety of emotion words, typically paired with images of corresponding facial expressions (see the My Feelings chart on the next page for an example).

Similar to the emotions wheel, this type of chart can help you identify and name what you're feeling by associating it with a visual. And since you can actually physically point to what you're feeling, it can also help you share what you're feeling with others (especially if you're having trouble finding the words!). Granted, these types of charts are inherently limiting because they don't showcase the full range of potential feelings, but they are an excellent jumping-off point.

Now for a story: One cold winter day at the preschool in rural Iowa, a kid who I

my feelings

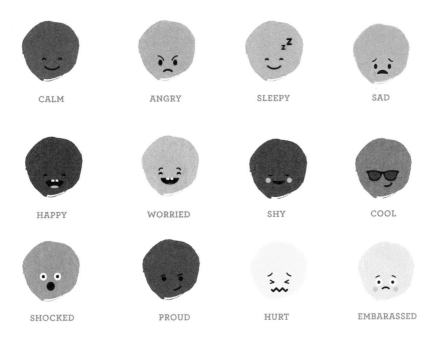

CALM

ANGRY

SLEEPY

SAD

HAPPY

WORRIED

SHY

COOL

SHOCKED

PROUD

HURT

EMBARASSED

would describe as rather quiet and reserved took my hand and made his way over to the feelings chart, where he pointed to the "worried" face. I read the word out loud to him and asked him if he could tell me more about what he was feeling. He said someone had just taken the wooden blocks he'd been using, and he was upset. I thanked him for sharing with me, let him know that it was OK to feel upset, and suggested we talk to the other child together. Spoiler: two minutes later the two kids were happily building a castle together. I love telling this story for several reasons. One: it's a beautiful example of someone finding a way to identify and feel their feelings, and

ultimately share them with someone else. Two: it shows us how tools like the emotions chart can be used in a real-life situation. Three: it's really, really adorable.

THE BAKING BY FEEL EMOTIONS WHEEL

OK, back to the wheel. Many variations of Plutchik's original emotions wheel have evolved in the decades since its creation, posing a variety of core and offshoot emotions.

In this book, I'm using the following core categories for my emotions wheel: happiness, sadness, anger, anxiety, and hope. I've mapped out sixty-five emotions,

lighthearted

in love

caring

trapped

confused

cheerful

feisty

content

joyful

excited

embarrassed

carefree

surprised

scared

nostalgic

grateful

impatient

proud

lost

restless

satisfied

relieved

silly

panicked

scattered

heartbroken

stressed

hopeless

overwhelmed

awkward

frazzled

FLAVORS OF

happy

FLAVORS OF

anxious

sorry

worried

FLAVORS OF

mad

homesick

FLAVORS OF

hopeful

inadequate

brave

doubtful

FLAVORS OF

sad

curious

discouraged

gloomy

adventurous

bored

confident

jealous

creative

rejected

motivated

lonely

sad

inspired

pessimistic

optimistic

sorrowful

which of course cannot fully account for the thousands of possible things you have the capacity to feel. But it's a place to start.

I know that it can seem pretty overwhelming to explore how you're feeling. It can be difficult, cathartic, liberating, and even painful. If you aren't sure of exactly what you're feeling in the moment, that's totally OK! The wheel is here as a tool to help you put names to the jumble of feelings.

HOW TO USE THE WHEEL

The emotions wheel helps us name our feelings by providing space for both specificity and complexity. For instance: typically, we're not *just* anxious. We might also be feeling lost, overwhelmed, and maybe a bit lonely too. Your emotional recipe is unique to you at this particular moment in time. You are a multidimensional human made up of messy, complex, and beautiful intricacies, and your feelings reflect that!

Start with the big bucket categories in the center of the wheel: happy, sad, mad, anxious, and hopeful. Once you've identified which broad category (or categories!) you think your current feelings might fit into, try going a bit deeper. Read through the second tier of emotions. Do any words from the outer circle jump out at you? Today it might be an instantaneous reaction of ah, yes, that's totally it! Or maybe nothing resonates right away. Take as much or as little time as you need. There's no pressure here. Feel free to take out a notebook and jot down some thoughts.

Yay for feeling our feelings. Now, let's get started!

emotional q & a

Before you get your hands covered in butter, grab your notebook and a pen/pencil/crayon/whatever. We're kicking things off with this super quick little Q & A. The answers are just for you. I promise no one's going to grade this—or anything else you do in this book. It's just a space to practice getting cozy with your feelings before you're busy frosting a cake or rolling out pie crust or taste-testing the cookie dough to make *absolutely sure* it's delicious.

So, let's get to it:

⁂ Which feelings feel the most familiar to you? To give a visual: which ones feel like those places on a staircase that have been worn down over time from a million footsteps?
⁂ Which ones feel sort of remote or unreachable?
⁂ Which do you have the most affection for?
⁂ The least?
⁂ Which feelings feel the most shareable?
⁂ The loneliest?
⁂ Do your feelings ever show up anywhere in your body? Where?
⁂ Last (and unrelated): If you were a cookie, what kind would you be? (I'm oatmeal chocolate chip, obviously.)

grounding activities

Grounding activities are actions that help to redirect your mind from thoughts that are stressing you out/making you sad/fueling your frustration/etc. They are practiced to help bring you into the present moment through engaging with your senses. Here's a list of some grounding activities you can try out at any point you're experiencing big feelings—while using this book or otherwise. With baking in particular, there's lots of time spent waiting for the timer to go off. Might as well use it to ground yourself!

* Go outside and feel the grass under your bare feet.
* Grab your coziest sweater and your fuzziest slippers and your fleecy-ist blanket.
* Draw in a coloring book using your art supply of choice.
* Drink a glass of (very cold) water or a mug of (hot but not too hot) tea.
* Go on a walk with the sole intention of viewing as many flowers as you can.
* Water your plants (but only if they need it— don't overwater on my account!).
* Do some yarn work. Crochet/knit yourself something warm.
* Put on your favorite playlist and break out the dance moves!
* Hug someone you like hugging.
* Run yourself a bath and focus on how the water feels on your skin. Bonus points for adding some Epsom salts.
* Do the dishes. Yes, really!
* Admire the way the light streams through your window.
* Do a quick visualization: I like to imagine a soft lavender-colored mist encircling my body with every exhale.
* Play catch.
* Close your eyes and feel the way the air moves across your skin.
* Do some stretches (butterfly pose, anyone?).
* Light your favorite candle (in my case, anything with notes of apple cider and cinnamon).
* And my favorite: sample what you're making! Pay attention to where you're tasting the flavor on your tongue. Does the flavor build, or hit you all at once? With flavor combos, can you detect which flavor comes first and which comes last? What's the texture like? Smooth? Crunchy? Thick? Creamy?

supplies

I promise you don't need a ton of supplies or tools to make the recipes in this book! But, if you were to make every single thing at the same time, this is the (almost) full list of what you'd need:

PANS

2 half-sheet baking pans

8-inch square cake pan

three 8-inch round cake pans

two 9-inch round cake pans

9 x 13-inch cake pan

9 x 5-inch loaf pan

12-cup Bundt pan

standard (12-cup) muffin tin

9-inch pie dish

TOOLS

digital scale

electric stand mixer (with paddle, whisk, and dough hook attachments) or hand mixer

candy thermometer (yes, you need it)

wire cooling racks

food processor

whisk

offset spatula

bench scraper (my fave tool!)

wooden spoon

flexible silicone spatula

chef's knife

zester

heatproof tongs

cutting board

measuring cups

measuring spoons

glass measuring cup (for liquids)

parchment paper

aluminum foil

kitchen scissors

cookie portion scoops—small, medium, and large

wooden skewers/toothpicks (for testing done-ness!)

BOWLS/STOVETOP ITEMS

heatproof metal bowl

mixing bowls (small, medium, and large)

heavy-bottomed saucepan

large cast-iron skillet or Dutch oven

PANTRY

all-purpose flour

cake flour

granulated sugar

brown sugar (dark and light)

powdered sugar

sanding sugar

turbinado sugar

toasted nuts (walnuts, pecans, almonds)

kosher salt

flaky salt

baking powder

baking soda

cocoa powder (Dutch-process and regular)

espresso powder

spices (especially cinnamon, cardamom, ginger, and nutmeg)

tapioca starch

cornstarch

vegetable oil

olive oil

extracts (vanilla, almond, maple, coconut)

honey

chocolate chips

semisweet chocolate

milk chocolate

lemons, limes, oranges

FRIDGE

unsalted butter (the #1 ingredient!)

large eggs

buttermilk

whole milk

heavy cream

sour cream

baking tips & tricks

SOME HELPFUL CONVERSIONS

1 cup all-purpose flour = 130g

1 cup cake flour = 130g

1 cup granulated sugar = 200g

1 cup brown sugar (light or dark) = 200g

1 cup powdered sugar = 120g

1 cup cocoa powder = 90g

1 cup graham cracker crumbs = 100g

1 cup butter = 227g (2 sticks)

1 cup cream cheese = 226g

1 cup peanut butter = 250g

1 whole egg = 50g

1 egg white = 35g

1 egg yolk = 15g

my "pinch" is ~ halfway between ⅛ and ¼ teaspoon

3 teaspoons = 1 tablespoon

4 tablespoons = ¼ cup

2 cups = 1 pint

1 pound = 455g

SOME NOTES ON WHAT ROOM TEMP
ACTUALLY MEANS

Using room temp ingredients, such as milk, eggs, or butter, is crucial in some recipes (especially some cake recipes!) because it allows the batter to properly combine and emulsify. This helps make sure your final product comes out with the right texture.

You'll know your butter is room temp when you can poke your finger into it easily to leave an impression but it doesn't turn into a melty greasy mess on your finger. Personally, I like to keep a couple of sticks of butter out on the counter at all times. But, a word of caution: do this only if your kitchen isn't too hot, because melty butter is not the vibe we're going for (unless I say so directly!).

It's much easier to separate egg whites from egg yolks when the eggs are cold. So if you need to separate your eggs and they also need to be room temp, go ahead and separate them straight from the fridge and then let them come to room temp. To separate an egg: grab two small bowls. Carefully crack the egg around the middle and then focus on gently transferring the yolk back and forth between the two halves of the shell, allowing the white to flow down into the first bowl waiting below. Once the white is separated out, transfer the yolk to the second bowl.

A QUICK TUTORIAL ON MEASURING

for flour:

Spoon and level, baby, spoon and level! We're definitely not trying to pack down as much flour as we can fit in the measuring cup (it's not brown sugar!)—we're lightly spooning our flour into the cup using a spoon, and then leveling off the excess. Try not to dip your measuring cup directly into the container of flour—you'll likely end up with too much. And even better—use a scale (more on that below).

for brown sugar (light or dark):

When I say 1 cup brown sugar, I mean 1 cup **packed** brown sugar. Press the sugar firmly down into the measuring cup and make sure you're filling the entire thing.

TRUST YOURSELF!

A big part of success in the kitchen is having confidence in yourself: your perception, your intuition, and your ability to connect with your senses.

- If your cookies already have that golden brown crisp around the edges a minute early, go ahead and pull 'em out.
- When you're browning your butter, use your nose. It'll smell quite nutty.
- If your dough feels too sticky when you're kneading, add that extra tablespoon of flour.

Basically, I'm (probably) not in your kitchen right now! In your kitchen, you're the expert. Feel it out.

A LIST OF REASONS TO BAKE BY WEIGHT

- You don't have to dig out the measuring cups—all you need is a scale and a bowl.
- It's more precise, so you'll never have to wonder if you're accidentally adding too much flour.
- It makes it super easy to cut recipes in half (even ones that come out to weird fractions like half of ⅓ cup, or ½ egg).
- You can get a scale for $15, but it feels fancy.

SOME NOTES ON INGREDIENTS

Light brown sugar and dark brown sugar are mostly interchangeable, but the swap can result in some slight changes in color and flavor. Light brown sugar is my general go-to, but since dark brown sugar has more molasses in it, I use it when I'm looking for a stronger flavor.

The vast majority of recipes in this book call for all-purpose flour, but there are a few that call for cake flour (when we're looking for a really soft and fluffy crumb). No prob if you don't have cake flour on hand—you can make your own with two ingredients! First: measure out 1 cup (130g) all-purpose flour. Remove 2 tablespoons of the all-purpose flour, then add 2 tablespoons cornstarch. Pass the mixture through a sifter or fine-mesh sieve to combine. Note: It's usually not a good idea to swap in cake flour when the recipe calls for all-purpose flour—those recipes may need the stronger structure from the higher protein content of all-purpose flour!

I like to use Gold Medal all-purpose flour, Domino 10x powdered sugar, and Diamond Crystal kosher salt. This one is the most important—please use Diamond, *not* Morton! Diamond salt grains are pyramid-shaped and hollow, making it lighter and more forgiving (you're less likely to oversalt!). If you do use Morton, you'll need to use less salt than the recipe calls for. Otherwise, I'm not too picky!

I always use large eggs. They should be ~ 50g each without the shell.

In this book, we use whole milk only—don't try to sneak in that skim.

SOME NOTES ABOUT FLAVORS

I don't believe in strictly relegating certain flavors to specific holidays or times of the year. If you want to eat pumpkin pie in August, that's fine. If you want snowball cookies in March, let's do it. The taste buds want what the taste buds want.

HOW TO TOAST NUTS

Several of the recipes in this book call for toasted nuts. Yes, toasting the nuts is an extra step, but the resulting flavor is really, really worth it. Here's what you do: Preheat the oven to 350°F and spread the nuts in a single layer on your baking sheet. Bake for 8 to 10 minutes, tossing the nuts around every couple of minutes to make sure everything toasts evenly. Let cool and use! And if you'd like to do it in advance (a planner, huh), just wait 'til they're cool, put 'em in a Ziploc bag, write the date on it, and toss in the freezer for up to six months.

HOW TO BROWN BUTTER

Heat a small skillet over medium heat. Add the butter and stir with a rubber spatula until the butter looks golden brown (*not* dark brown!) and smells nutty. Watch it carefully and remove it from the heat as soon as it reaches a deep caramel color.

A NOTE ON PIE CRUST/MAKING YOUR LIFE EASIER

If you want to really impress your future self, make a few batches of pie crust at once and pop the dough disks in your freezer so they'll be ready to use at your leisure. Truly, there are few things that thrill me more than making a pie with homemade crust that's premade and ready to go! They'll keep in the freezer (in a Ziploc freezer bag, wrapped tightly in plastic wrap) for up to 3 months. When you're ready to use a frozen crust: pop it in the fridge overnight (if you're a planning type), or out on the counter for about 20 minutes (if you're a fly-by-the-seat-of-your-pants kind of person, like me), then proceed with the recipe.

ready, set, bake!

Let's talk about how to set ourselves up to bake with minimal interruption/stress.

First, read the entire recipe before you begin. You don't have to pore over every word. A little it's-ten-minutes-before-class-starts-and-you-haven't-done-the-reading-yet speed reading is OK. But giving it a glance over helps you know what to expect.

Then, turn on the oven. Did you know ovens need to preheat for like half an hour to get to and stay at the right temp? Fire that baby up.

Next, grab all the tools you'll need and put 'em out on the counter within easy reach. Rubber spatula? Check. Measuring spoons? Check. Whatever else I tell you you'll need? Check.

Now, measure out and prep all of your ingredients. A little mise en place, if you will. *Psst: mise en place is a French culinary term that refers to the act of putting everything in its place before you start.* This means the ingredients are measured, the pans are covered in parchment paper, the oven is on, and your whisk is at the ready. Basically, it makes our baking lives easier. Some might argue that you're creating more dishes to wash with this method, but to me it truly is preferable to have everything visible and ready before you start mixing away. That way, you won't be making your favorite oatmeal cookies and go to grab your giant glass container of flour with slippery butter-coated hands and end up dropping it on the floor where it shatters into many pieces and you have to drag the giant vacuum out of the closet to clean it up (if it sounds like this highly specific example comes from personal experience, that's because it does).

OK! Let's bake!

happy

The recipes in this chapter are here to help you celebrate, both the big and little things.

Vibes: Summertime sunshine, the right number of candles on your birthday cake, pleasant butterflies in your stomach

This is definitely a delicious section of the book. I mean, every section of this book is delicious, but there's something especially magical about tasting really good food when you're in a great mood. For me, it kind of feels like my taste buds amplify and my ability to enjoy increases by like 40 percent at least. There tends to be a lot of *mmm*s and *omg*s and "Wow, I actually really am a good cook!"s coming out of my mouth.

These are some of the most desirable feelings—the ones we chase after and try to hold on to for as long as possible. Feelings can be fleeting, so I sometimes find myself wanting to bottle these up to save for later. That's of course not possible (yet!), but there are some next-best-thing options. You could try writing down (in more detail than you think you need) the particular nuances of the joy/excitement/love/etc. that you're feeling in this particular moment. You could establish a keepsake box where you store sentimental things. You could snap a picture and save it to a special album on your phone (mine's titled "sparkly moments"—yes, I'm serious). I love how many beautiful permutations of happiness there are. There's the happiness that comes from sharing something with other people, and the kind that comes entirely from within. The triumphant sort, the relaxed sort, the belly laugh sort. Whichever variation you're feeling at the moment, I'm delighted for you.

Many of the "happy" recipes are brightly flavored to match the brightness of your mood. Some are comforting. Some are meant for sharing. They're all meant to keep the good vibes flowing and complement the sweetness of life. They're all about enjoyment. I urge you to give yourself the time and space to really savor these feelings (and desserts!) decadently. You without a doubt deserve it.

happy

carefree

caring

cheerful

content

delighted

excited

grateful

feisty

in love

joyful

nostalgic

lighthearted

playful

proud

relieved

satisfied

silly

surprised

YOU MIGHT BE FEELING:
*the kind of laid-back most often
found lounging on a beach*

You might be having a moment where you're not super worried about things you need to do—both for yourself and for others. It can be super hard to let go of all those worries, so I love that you're cutting yourself a break. Real quick: do a mini scan of your body. But instead of looking for places of tension, try noticing what already feels relaxed. Maybe you notice that your shoulders are relaxed down your back, your jaw is unclenched, and the space between your eyebrows is un-scrunched. Yay for calm bodies and calm minds. Now, to really indulge in this feeling, take a minute to close your eyes and imagine yourself walking through a field of wildflowers as high as your waist. Feel the flowers brush against your skin, a light breeze blowing past you, and the sunshine warming your cheeks. Stay here for as long as feels right, then gently open your eyes.

OK, I'll stop bossing you around now, I promise—go ahead and bake your pie.

spiced french silk pie

MAKES A 9-INCH PIE

I'm a Midwesterner, and (many) Midwesterners love French silk pie. This is a spin on the classic recipe, dressed up with some warming spices that play nicely with the delicate sweetness of the silky filling. I wouldn't call it a *simple* recipe, but it's worth the effort. And sometimes the lighthearted challenge of crafting a sort of complex, multistep dessert is a great match for a carefree mood. I first fell in love with the chocolate + cayenne + nutmeg pairing when I worked at a bean-to-bar chocolate company, and trust me—it just works. If you've never eaten a French silk pie before, you can expect a smooth, silky, almost mousse-like (but thicker) chocolate filling with a flaky all-butter crust and a fluffy layer of whipped cream on the top.

FOR THE CRUST

1 recipe Single Pie crust (page 238)

FOR THE WHIPPED CREAM

1½ cups cold heavy cream

2 tablespoons powdered sugar

1 teaspoon vanilla extract

FOR THE FILLING

6 oz (170g) chopped bittersweet chocolate

½ teaspoon kosher salt

⅛ teaspoon cayenne

a pinch of ground nutmeg

4 room temp large eggs

1 cup (200g) granulated sugar, divided

½ cup (1 stick, 113g) room temp unsalted butter

2½ teaspoons vanilla extract

the how-to: crust

1 Preheat the oven to 375°F.

2 Roll out your pie crust to an 11-inch circle. Transfer the dough to a 9-inch pie plate. Fold the excess under (it might take a couple of folds) so the edge of the crust lines up with the edge of the pie plate. Prick the bottom of the crust all over with a fork. Freeze it for 30 minutes.

3 Place a piece of parchment paper inside the pie crust and fill it with pie weights or dried beans. Place the pie plate on a rimmed baking sheet. Bake for 25 minutes. Remove the pie weights, return the crust to the oven, and bake for 10 to 15 minutes more, until light golden brown. Set aside on a wire rack to cool completely. Turn off the oven.

the how-to: whipped cream

In the bowl of a stand mixer fitted with the whisk attachment, beat the heavy cream, powdered sugar, and vanilla extract on medium-high speed until stiff peaks form, about 3 minutes. Transfer the whipped cream to a medium bowl, cover with plastic wrap, and put it in the fridge for later. Wipe out the stand mixer bowl and set it aside.

the how-to: filling

1 In a medium saucepan, bring 2 inches of water to a gentle simmer. Place the chopped chocolate in a medium heatproof bowl set over the simmering water—make sure the bottom of the bowl isn't touching the water! Hold on to the side of the bowl with an oven-mittened hand. Stir the chocolate constantly with a rubber spatula until melted. Remove the bowl from the heat. Add the salt, cayenne, and nutmeg. Whisk until smooth. Set aside to cool.

2 Put the eggs and ½ cup (100g) of the granulated sugar in a second medium heatproof bowl (or wipe out the first one!) and whisk until smooth. Place the bowl over the gently simmering water. Again, hold on to the side of the bowl with an oven-mittened hand. Stir continuously (Really, continuously! We don't want our eggs to scramble!) with a spatula until the egg mixture reaches 160°F when measured with a candy or instant-read cooking thermometer (about 5 minutes if you don't have a thermometer). Remove it from the heat and set aside to cool for at least 20 minutes.

3 In the bowl of a stand mixer fitted with the paddle attachment, cream together the butter and the remaining ½ cup (100g) of granulated sugar on medium-high speed until light and fluffy, about 3 minutes. Switch to the whisk attachment. Add the cooled egg mixture and the vanilla extract. Beat on medium-high speed until fluffy, about 5 minutes. Add the cooled melted chocolate mixture and beat on medium-high speed for 2 more minutes. Using a spatula, gently fold in 1 cup of the chilled whipped cream mixture.

4 Plop the chocolate mixture into the prepared pie crust and spread it out into an even layer. Chill for at least 4 hours. Top with the rest of the whipped cream just before serving. Store in the fridge, covered, for up to 2 days.

You likely don't hear this enough, so say it with me: I'm a really great [friend, partner, parent, coworker, sibling, neighbor, caretaker, fill in others I missed here]. Now, let's talk about how amazing it is that you're able to tune in to other people's needs and offer them support. It takes a lot of strength to be there for someone through both the fun times and rough ones, and it's also one of the most important expressions of love.

But: caretaking can also be exhausting. So while you're busy caring for everyone else, don't forget to care for *you*. And here I'm not talking like "do a moisturizing face mask." I'm talking about recognizing when you need a break and taking it, making your mental health and emotional well-being a priority, and allowing yourself to accept care and help from others. Remember, you deserve the same level of care that you give other people!

mini limey olive oil cakes

MAKES 12 MINI CAKES

These cakes just feel *fancy*. They've got richness from the olive oil, brightness from the lime zest/juice, and just a bit of crunch on the outside from the cornmeal. By baking the batter as individual cakes in a muffin tin, we're able to get more of the crunchy edge of the cake texture in each bite, which is my favorite part of olive oil cakes. But of course, the incredibly moist center isn't something to be scoffed at either.

These come together quickly (no mixer required!) but look and taste like a labor of love. They're the perfect little treat to show someone you care. And the best part: everyone gets their own individual cake.

FOR THE CAKES

1¼ cups (163g) all-purpose flour

½ cup (80g) fine or medium grind cornmeal

1½ teaspoons baking powder

¾ teaspoon kosher salt

2 tablespoons fresh lime zest

1¼ cups (250g) granulated sugar

1 cup extra virgin olive oil

3 large eggs

2 tablespoons fresh lime juice

FOR THE GLAZE

1 cup (120g) powdered sugar

2 tablespoons + 1 teaspoon fresh lime juice

a couple drops of vanilla extract

the how-to: cakes

1. Preheat the oven to 350°F and thoroughly grease a standard 12-cup muffin tin (no muffin liners needed!).

2. In a medium bowl, whisk together the flour, cornmeal, baking powder, and salt.

3. Put the granulated sugar in a large bowl, then rub the lime zest into the sugar using your fingertips (this will help release more flavor from the zest!). Add the olive oil, eggs, and lime juice and whisk until combined. Pour the dry ingredients into the wet ingredients and mix with a rubber spatula until just combined.

4. Spoon the batter evenly into the prepared muffin cups (I like to use a cookie scoop for this). Bake for 20 to 22 minutes, until golden. As soon as the cakes are cool enough to handle, pop them out of the pan and place them onto the cooling rack upside down (yes, these will be eaten upside down!).

the how-to: glaze

In a small bowl, whisk together the powdered sugar, lime juice, and vanilla extract. Drizzle the glaze over the warm cakes. Wait a bit for the glaze to set before serving. Store at room temp in an airtight container for up to 3 days.

I'd define my personal brand of cheerfulness as a bright and bouncy sense of waking up on the right side of the bed. It's a mood that's a great match for baking! But really, it's a great match for any number of activities. I find that a cheerful mood helps me enjoy simple pleasures, and not worry too much about my never-ending to-do list. I hope you're taking a little break from your list as well.

I love how a cheerful mood feels almost contagious. So spread your infectious, joyous cheer widely. Psst: baking a highly shareable triple-layer cake will definitely help with that.

lemon poppy seed cake

MAKES AN 8-INCH 3-LAYER CAKE

It seems like every time I'm in the airport I somehow end up with a giant, plastic-wrapped, decidedly not-fresh lemon poppy seed muffin. I have a very clear mental image of the crumbs getting everywhere while I try to scarf it down in the five minutes before I have to board the plane. So if you, like me, associate this flavor combo with the unfortunate pairing of fluorescent lighting and a vague sense of disappointment, I hope this cake will give you some new associations.

Here, I've taken the lemon poppy seed muffin concept and reconfigured it into a light and refreshing three-layer cake. We start out with a moist vanilla cake, flavored with a healthy dose of fresh lemon—both zest and juice. Then we add poppy seeds to the frosting for a deep and rich flavor to complement the tang of the cream cheese (also, a texture boost!).

This recipe is essentially the embodiment of cheerfulness in cake form. It doesn't get much sunnier than a triple-layer lemon cake!

FOR THE CAKES

3½ cups (455g) all-purpose flour
2½ teaspoons baking powder
½ teaspoon baking soda
1 teaspoon kosher salt
1 cup room temp heavy cream
¼ cup fresh lemon juice

½ cup (120g) room temp sour cream

2 teaspoons vanilla extract

2 cups (400g) granulated sugar

2 tablespoons fresh lemon zest

1½ cups (3 sticks, 340g) room temp unsalted
butter

4 room temp large eggs

FOR THE POPPY SEED CREAM CHEESE FROSTING

¾ cup (1½ sticks, 170g) room temp unsalted
butter

one 8-oz package (226g) room temp cream
cheese

4 cups (480g) powdered sugar

2 teaspoons vanilla extract

a pinch of kosher salt

2 tablespoons poppy seeds

the how-to: cake

1   Preheat the oven to 350°F. Line three
8-inch round cake pans with parchment
paper. Grease the pans with butter.

2   In a large bowl, whisk together the flour,
baking powder, baking soda, and salt. In a
small bowl or liquid measuring cup, whisk
together the heavy cream, lemon juice,
sour cream, and vanilla extract.

3   Put the granulated sugar in the bowl of a
stand mixer, then rub the lemon zest into
the sugar using your fingertips (this will
help release more flavor from the zest!).
Using the paddle attachment, cream
together the butter and lemon sugar on
medium-high speed until very light and
fluffy, about 3 minutes. Scrape down the
bowl. With the mixer on medium speed,
add the eggs, one at a time, and mix until
thoroughly combined. Reduce the speed

to medium-low. With the mixer running,
add the dry ingredient mixture and wet
ingredient mixture in three alternating
batches, starting and ending with the
dry ingredients. Give the batter a good
stir with a rubber spatula, scraping the
bottom and sides of the bowl to make sure
everything's combined.

4   Divide the batter evenly among your
prepared pans. Bake for 28 to 30 minutes,
until golden and a tester inserted in the
middle of a layer comes out with moist
crumbs. Cool for 10 minutes in the pan,
then turn the layers out onto wire racks to
cool completely.

**the how-to: poppy seed cream cheese
frosting**

In the bowl of a stand mixer fitted with the
paddle attachment, beat the butter and cream
cheese on medium-high speed until light and
fluffy, about 3 minutes. Slowly beat in the
powdered sugar on medium speed. Add the
vanilla extract, salt, and poppy seeds and beat
until combined.

the how-to: assembly

Level the cakes, fill, and frost with an offset
spatula. Store in the fridge for up to 2 days.

YOU MIGHT BE FEELING:
*a sense of well-being, like
you just got a big hug
from your grandma*

It can be so challenging to fully (or even mostly!) exist in the moment. For so much of the time, we're living in the future or the past (shout-out to both my worriers and my ruminators). So it's pretty amazing that right now, you're in the here and now.

Baking is one of those activities that grounds me in the present. And that's basically the whole point of this book! But since you're already feeling in the groove: let's keep this here and get the vibe going. Before we do, could you grab your journal and make a quick little bullet-point list of some things you like about yourself? It'll be there for you to revisit later, when you need a boost.

peanut butter crunch cookies

MAKES ABOUT 22 COOKIES

I don't know about you, but there's something about peanut butter cookies that makes me feel like all's right with the world (at least for the next few bites). It's a comforting cookie.

There are many schools of thought about what makes a peanut butter cookie a good peanut butter cookie. Should it be soft or crunchy? The size of your hand or bite-sized? Smooth peanut butter or chunky peanut butter? Decoratively patterned with the tines of a fork, or just dropped on the baking sheet as is? This recipe showcases my favorite kind: thick and chewy with some chopped honey-roasted peanuts mixed in for a bit of crunch. And definitely, definitely decoratively patterned with the tines of a fork.

2½ cups (325g) all-purpose flour

1 teaspoon baking soda

½ teaspoon kosher salt

1 cup (2 sticks, 227g) room temp unsalted butter

1 cup (250g) creamy peanut butter (not natural)

1 cup (200g) dark brown sugar

1 large egg

2 teaspoons vanilla extract

1 cup (140g) honey-roasted peanuts

the how-to

1 Preheat the oven to 350°F and line a baking sheet with parchment paper.

2 In a medium bowl, whisk together the flour, baking soda, and salt.

3 In the bowl of a stand mixer fitted with the paddle attachment, cream together the butter, peanut butter, and brown sugar on medium-high speed until creamy, about 2 minutes. Beat in the egg and vanilla extract. With the mixer running on low speed, add the flour mixture and mix until the dough comes together. Add the peanuts and mix on low speed just until combined.

4 Form the dough into 2-tablespoon (40g) sized balls. Roll each ball in the granulated sugar, completely covering all of the surfaces. Press the dough balls down lightly in a crisscross pattern using the tines of a fork.

5 Place the cookies at least 2 inches apart on your prepared baking sheet. Bake for 11 to 12 minutes, until set. Let the cookies cool on the pan for 2 minutes, then transfer them to a wire rack to cool. Store at room temp in an airtight container for up to 3 days.

note: Yes, get the honey-roasted kind of peanuts!

It's no accident that delicious and delighted are etymologically similar. (Are they? They sound like it at the very least!) Delight feels like pure sunshine. Sometimes when I feel delighted I can almost feel the sunshine on my skin—even on a cold, dreary, and gray winter day.

Delight helps you exist in the present moment. It allows you to focus on what's going on in front of you—what a miracle that you exist right at this very second, with these very people, in this very place. I don't believe in a blanket view of gratitude—some things just plain suck and not everything's a lesson. But I also think that it's essential to stop and notice those sparkly moments of delight, no matter how fleeting.

So if you want to, pull out your journal and jot down what's delighted you today (don't forget to write down the date!). Now let's whip up something yum to keep the delighted times coming.

yellow cake with chocolate cream cheese frosting

MAKES AN 8-INCH SINGLE LAYER CAKE

It's important for you to know that I am a birthday person. In my family, we get entire birthday weeks. During your birthday week, you are the boss. You choose what to eat, what to watch, what to do. For the week, your silliest, most luxurious, even most obnoxious whims are embraced (OK, sometimes just tolerated). So when I tell you that this recipe is the one I use for my own birthday cake, you have to understand that I truly love it.

I'm of the opinion that there's no better combo than fluffy yellow cake + chocolate frosting. But this recipe takes it even further by turning that plain old chocolate frosting into chocolate *cream cheese* frosting. It's a delightful pairing, perfect for a delightful day.

FOR THE CAKE

1 cup (130g) cake flour

1 teaspoon baking powder

¼ teaspoon kosher salt

¼ cup (60g) sour cream

¼ cup heavy cream

½ cup (1 stick, 113g) room temp unsalted butter

¾ cup (150g) granulated sugar

1 large egg

2 large egg yolks

1½ teaspoons vanilla extract

2 oz (57g) melted and cooled semisweet
   chocolate

4 tablespoons (½ stick, 57g) room temp unsalted
   butter

4 oz (113g) room temp cream cheese

2 cups (240g) powdered sugar

2 tablespoons Dutch-process cocoa powder

a tiny pinch of kosher salt

the how-to: cake

1 Preheat the oven to 350°F and line the
   bottom of an 8-inch round cake pan with
   parchment paper. Grease the pan and
   parchment paper.

2 In a medium bowl, whisk together the flour,
   baking powder, and salt.

3 In a glass measuring cup or small bowl, stir
   together the sour cream and heavy cream.

4 In the bowl of a stand mixer fitted with the
   paddle attachment, cream together the
   butter and granulated sugar on medium-
   high speed for about 3 minutes, until very
   light and fluffy. Scrape down the bottom
   and sides of the bowl. Beat in the egg
   and egg yolks, one at a time, on medium-
   high speed until thoroughly combined.
   Continue beating for an additional 3
   minutes. Add the vanilla extract and mix
   on medium speed until combined. With the
   mixer running on low speed, add the flour
   mixture and sour cream mixture in two
   alternating batches, starting and ending
   with the flour.

5 Pour the batter into your prepared pan and
   smooth the top. Bake for 35 to 38 minutes,
   until a tester inserted in the center comes
   out with moist (but not wet!) crumbs.

Cool for 10 minutes in the pan, then turn
the cake out onto a wire rack to cool
completely.

6 While the cake is in the oven, melt the
   chocolate for your frosting—I like to do this
   by microwaving it in 30-second increments
   in a heatproof bowl, stirring in between.
   Set it aside to cool completely.

the how-to: frosting

1 In a stand mixer fitted with the paddle
   attachment, beat the butter and cream
   cheese on medium speed until smooth and
   fluffy, about 3 minutes. With the mixer
   running on low speed, gradually beat in
   the powdered sugar. Increase the speed
   to medium and beat until fluffy, about 2
   minutes. Add the melted chocolate, cocoa
   powder, and salt and beat on medium
   speed until thoroughly combined.

2 Using an offset spatula, frost the tops and
   sides of the cake with decorative swooshes!
   Store in an airtight container in the fridge
   for up to 2 days.

funnel cake with strawberry sauce

MAKES ABOUT FOUR 8-INCH FUNNEL CAKES

When I was little, my mom used to take my brother and sister and me to the River Market in downtown Kansas City on weekend mornings. For a visual, think of your local farmer's market, except approximately twelve times as large and year-round. There was so much to see (and taste!)—colorful vegetables, tons of flavors of honey sticks, brown speckled eggs. I loved it. But the very best part of it all was the gooey/crunchy, sticky, incredibly sweet funnel cake we'd share at the end. There's just something so exciting about a funnel cake. Even now, I'm filled with a particular sense of joy that I associate with eating them as a child.

You might be thinking, *Um, can you even make funnel cakes at home? Don't you need a deep fryer? Wouldn't that be really hard?* I'm here to tell you that yes, you can make them at home, no, you don't need a deep fryer, and no—it really isn't hard! All you'll need is a good amount of oil, a pastry bag/Ziploc with the end cut off, and some confidence.

FOR THE STRAWBERRY SAUCE

1 cup (168g) coarsely chopped fresh strawberries
1 teaspoon fresh lemon zest
2 tablespoons light brown sugar
2 tablespoons water

about 2 cups shortening/vegetable oil
  (for frying)

1½ cups (195g) all-purpose flour

¼ teaspoon kosher salt

1½ teaspoons baking powder

¼ teaspoon ground nutmeg

1 teaspoon fresh lemon zest

2 tablespoons light brown sugar

1 large egg

½ cup whole milk

½ cup water

½ teaspoon vanilla extract

½ cup (60g) powdered sugar, for coating

the how-to: strawberry sauce

Combine the strawberries, lemon zest, brown sugar, and water in a small saucepan over medium heat. Cook, stirring, until the strawberries are mostly broken down and the mixture is thick and syrupy, 5 to 7 minutes. Remove from the heat and set aside to cool.

the how-to: funnel cakes

1   Line a metal cooling rack with paper towels and set it over a rimmed baking sheet.

2   Heat the shortening or vegetable oil in an 8- or 10-inch skillet over medium-high heat until a candy thermometer reads 365°F. The shortening/oil should be about 1 inch deep.

3   While your oil is heating, make your batter. In a small bowl, whisk together the flour, salt, baking powder, nutmeg, and lemon zest.

4   In a medium bowl, whisk together the brown sugar, egg, milk, water, and vanilla extract. Add the dry ingredients and stir with a rubber spatula until just combined.

5   Transfer the batter into your squeeze bottle or plastic bag. If using a plastic bag, cut an ⅛-inch hole in one corner after putting the batter in—make sure to hold the bag with the hole facing up to avoid any leaks. Important note: Make sure to wear an apron and stand a safe distance back from the stove in case the oil splatters a bit! Squeeze the batter out in thin overlapping streams, all over the pan. This does not need to be pretty—you're looking for a maze of batter. Fry for about 1½ minutes on the first side, until golden. Flip over using heatproof tongs, then fry for 1 more minute on the other side. Carefully transfer the funnel cake to your prepared cooling rack to drain. Repeat with the remaining batter—you should end up with about four funnel cakes.

the how-to: assembly

Once you're finished frying all of the cakes, shower them very liberally with the powdered sugar. Top with dollops of the strawberry mixture. Pretend you're five. Eat immediately—these don't keep.

FEISTY

~~~

YOU MIGHT BE FEELING:
*like ruffling some feathers/
having some fun*

~~~

I know that feisty is often used in a dismissive or pejorative way, particularly if you're a woman. But here, I mean it in a truly appreciative way. I love that you're expressing yourself. Maybe you told someone what you needed today, even if it was hard. Maybe you stood up for a friend. Maybe you made out with that cute and incredibly kind person you went out with last night. What an achievement to unapologetically take up space and go after what you want.

double chocolate frosted cookies

~~~

MAKES ABOUT 40 COOKIES

This cookie recipe is paired with *feisty* because it's just a vibe match. I mean, there's definitely something *passionate* about the phrase "double chocolate." Psst: the double comes from the addition of cocoa powder and chopped semisweet chocolate. Here we're taking a standard chocolate cookie dough recipe and adding a couple of ingredients that add an element of intrigue: Dutch-process cocoa powder and coconut oil. The Dutch-process cocoa powder adds a rich and smooth flavor. The coconut oil creates a silky texture. These little dudes are bite-sized and topped with a swirl of simple chocolate buttercream. Adding some colorful sprinkles on top is encouraged.

FOR THE COOKIES

2 cups (260g) all-purpose flour

½ cup (45g) Dutch-process cocoa powder

½ teaspoon baking powder

½ teaspoon kosher salt

¾ cup (150g) granulated sugar

½ cup (1 stick, 113g) room temp unsalted butter

½ cup (100g) room temp (not melted!) coconut oil

1 large egg

1 teaspoon vanilla extract

5 oz (142g) chopped semisweet chocolate

FOR THE FROSTING

½ cup (1 stick, 113g) room temp unsalted butter

1¾ cups (210g) powdered sugar

¼ cup (25g) Dutch-process cocoa powder

2 tablespoons whole milk

1 teaspoon vanilla extract

the how-to: cookies

1 Preheat the oven to 375°F and line a baking sheet with parchment paper.

2 In a medium bowl, whisk together the flour, cocoa powder, baking powder, and salt.

3 In the bowl of a stand mixer fitted with the paddle attachment, cream together the granulated sugar, butter, and coconut oil on medium-high speed until very creamy, about 3 minutes. Beat in the egg and vanilla extract on medium speed until combined. Add the flour mixture and mix on low speed until just combined. Stir in the chopped chocolate with a rubber spatula. Scrape the bottom of the bowl with the spatula to make sure everything's all mixed in.

4 Roll the dough into 1-tablespoon (20g) sized balls. Place them 2 inches apart on your prepared baking sheet and flatten slightly using your palm or a glass.

5 Bake for 8 to 9 minutes, until the center is set. Let the cookies sit on the pan for 2 minutes, then transfer them to a cooling rack. Cool completely before frosting.

the how-to: frosting & assembly

While the cookies are baking, make your frosting. In the bowl of a stand mixer fitted with the paddle attachment, beat the butter on medium-high speed until creamy, about 2 minutes. With the mixer running on low, slowly add in the powdered sugar. Increase the speed to medium-high and beat until very fluffy, about 3 minutes. Beat in the cocoa powder, milk, and vanilla extract. When the cookies have cooled completely, frost the tops using an offset spatula. Store at room temp in an airtight container for up to 3 days.

YOU MIGHT BE FEELING:
like you're exactly where you're supposed to be, with the person you're supposed to be with

~~~~~~~

Sometimes we're moving so fast through life that we miss what's going on around us. So I'm really happy that today you stopped to smell the flowers.

I know this is kind of a cliché, but I actually get a lot out of taking time to notice what I'm grateful for. My first year in college I wrote down something I was grateful for on a Post-it note every day and posted it on my dorm wall. By the end, there were so many Post-its that I could hardly see the dingy white-painted cinder block dorm wall (thank god). It was helpful to have a physical record of the good things going on in my life in a big and vaguely scary transition year. And though I couldn't really remember the details of each day, I could go back and see at least one thing I liked about each one.

Give it a shot! Jot down what you're grateful for today in your journal (don't forget to date it!).

butterscotch pudding pie

MAKES A 9-INCH PIE

My grandma made a variation of this butterscotch pie for every holiday, event, or family get-together I can remember when I was growing up. It's a treasured family recipe. A classic. Being a busy woman, her version involved boxed pudding mix and a store-bought graham cracker crust. What we're making here is essentially the same deal, but from scratch! I suspect you'll end up agreeing with me that it's worth the extra time and effort.

FOR THE CRUST

1¼ cups (150g) graham cracker crumbs

2 tablespoons dark brown sugar

¼ teaspoon ground cinnamon

6 tablespoons (85g) melted unsalted butter

FOR THE FILLING

¾ cup (150g) dark brown sugar

3 tablespoons water

1 cup heavy cream

¾ cup whole milk

1 teaspoon kosher salt

4 large egg yolks

3 tablespoons cornstarch

4 tablespoons (½ stick, 57g) unsalted butter, chopped into ½-inch cubes

2 teaspoons vanilla extract

1 tablespoon bourbon (optional)

½ cup heavy cream

1 tablespoon powdered sugar

the how-to: crust

1　Preheat the oven to 350°F.

2　In a medium bowl, combine the graham cracker crumbs, brown sugar, and cinnamon. Stir in the melted butter. Press the crust firmly into the bottom and sides of a 9-inch pie plate (I find it helps to use the bottom of a measuring cup or glass). Place the pie plate on a rimmed baking sheet and bake for 10 to 12 minutes, until lightly golden. Set aside on a wire rack to cool while you make the filling. Turn off the oven.

the how-to: filling

1　Combine the brown sugar and water in a medium heavy-bottomed pot with a candy thermometer clipped to the side. Cook the mixture over medium heat until the sugar dissolves and the bubbling mixture reaches the soft-boil stage (240°F), about 6 minutes. Just hang tight and don't stir.

2　Remove the saucepan from the heat and whisk in the heavy cream, whole milk, and salt. It will foam up a bit here—make sure to step back!

3　Temper the eggs: In a medium heatproof bowl, whisk together the egg yolks and cornstarch. Carefully scoop out ½ cup of the hot butterscotch mixture from the saucepan (I use a ladle for this). Slowly drizzle the ½ cup of butterscotch mixture into the egg yolk mixture, whisking constantly. Pour the tempered egg yolk mixture into the saucepan containing the rest of the butterscotch, whisking. Turn

the heat back on to medium and whisk constantly until the mixture comes to a simmer. Cook the simmering mixture, whisking constantly, for 2 to 3 minutes, until it thickens. Turn off the heat, add the butter, vanilla, and bourbon (if using), and whisk until combined.

4　Pour the filling into your prepared pie plate. Transfer it to the fridge to cool completely, at least 3 hours.

the how-to: whipped cream & assembly

1　Once the pie is completely chilled, start the whipped cream. In the bowl of a stand mixer fitted with the whisk attachment, beat the heavy cream and powdered sugar on medium-high speed until soft peaks form, about 3 minutes.

2　Just before serving, plop the whipped cream on top of the cooled pie and spread it out into an even layer using an offset spatula. Store in the fridge, covered, for up to 2 days.

YOU MIGHT BE FEELING:
*as if your soul found a
match and a flame was lit*

Falling in love requires an incredible amount of risk-taking and vulnerability. You have to put yourself out there, be willing to take a chance, open your heart, and learn a new way of being with someone. It's pretty amazing that you ended up here, with this person, at this time. Everyone experiences love differently, but for me, I might describe it as noticing a sparkle in someone's eyes that makes my stomach feel like it flipped upside down. You might want to know what third grade was like for them, or put on your favorite movie just to watch their face during your favorite parts.

But there's also the part of love that comes later: being in love. I associate this with feeling seen and known. Knowing for sure that your person's love isn't based on the softened, just-met version of yourself, but a series of shared and messy experiences/misunderstandings/joys. Doing something kind like picking up their dry cleaning, even though you're so annoyed right now you forgot why you live here. A deep kind of support and care.

I've highlighted a couple of types of "in love" here, but I also want to honor that there are an infinite number of ways to love! Whatever your "in love" feels like today, I love it.

strawberries & chocolate cookies

MAKES 24 COOKIES

OK, yes, the strawberry and chocolate combo is a little cliché. But it's cliché for a reason— it's delicious. These cookies can fit a variety of situations, including: making them for someone you just met but have texted five of your friends about: "Oh, I just happened to be making a batch of cookies and thought you might want them all!," or for someone you've been partnered with for the past [any number of!] years: "I know you had a hard week, so I made these to eat together tonight while watching the 'Dinner Party' episode of *The Office* for the twenty-second time."

They are deliciously pillow-like, speckled with juicy pieces of fresh strawberries and puddles of chopped chocolate throughout. Basically, you get chocolate-covered strawberries without all the hassle.

2½ cups (325g) all-purpose flour

1 teaspoon baking soda

1 teaspoon cream of tartar

½ teaspoon kosher salt

1 cup (2 sticks, 227g) room temp unsalted butter

1⅓ cups (267g) granulated sugar

1 large egg

1½ teaspoons vanilla extract

½ cup (84g) coarsely chopped fresh strawberries

4 oz (113g) coarsely chopped semisweet chocolate or white chocolate

the how-to:

1 Preheat the oven to 350°F and line a baking sheet with parchment paper.

2 In a medium bowl, whisk together the flour, baking soda, cream of tartar, and salt.

3 In the bowl of a stand mixer fitted with the paddle attachment, cream together the butter and granulated sugar on medium-high speed until light and fluffy, about 2 minutes. Beat in the egg and vanilla extract. Mix in the flour mixture on low speed. Scrape the bottom of the bowl with a spatula to make sure everything's all mixed in. Add the strawberries and chopped chocolate and stir with a rubber spatula until combined. Scoop into 2-tablespoon (40g) balls and arrange 3 inches apart on the cookie sheet.

4 Bake for 11 to 13 minutes, until the cookies are set and the edges are lightly golden. Let cool on the pan for 2 minutes, then transfer them to a wire rack to cool completely. Store at room temp in an airtight container for up to 2 days.

molasses gingersnaps

MAKES 30 COOKIES

Molasses cookies are often maligned as the last choice, vaguely yucky option at the holiday dessert table. I've had many less than stellar molasses cookies myself. So I get your hesitation if you turned to "joyful" and thought: "No, there cannot possibly be anything joyous about a molasses cookie." But these little soft and chewy bites of heaven (an exaggeration, but still) might change your mind. We've got the usual spices: cinnamon and ginger, and, of course, the molasses, but we also have a healthy dose of fresh lemon zest that brightens up the whole thing and transforms it almost into a new cookie. Yes, they can be eaten warm.

FOR THE COOKIES

½ cup (1 stick, 113g) unsalted butter
2 cups (260g) all-purpose flour
2 teaspoons baking soda
1 teaspoon ground cinnamon
½ teaspoon ground ginger
1 teaspoon fresh lemon zest
½ teaspoon kosher salt
½ cup (100g) granulated sugar
¼ cup (50g) light brown sugar
1 large egg
¼ cup (80g) molasses (not blackstrap)

FOR THE TOPPING

⅓ cup (66g) granulated sugar
¼ teaspoon ground cinnamon

the how-to

1 Preheat the oven to 375°F and line a baking sheet with parchment paper.

2 Brown your butter (see page 16) and set aside to cool slightly.

3 In a medium bowl, whisk together the flour, baking soda, cinnamon, ginger, lemon zest, and salt. In a large bowl, whisk together the granulated sugar, brown sugar, browned butter, egg, and molasses. Pour the dry ingredients into the wet ingredients and mix with a rubber spatula until combined.

4 In a small bowl, combine the topping ingredients.

5 Form the dough into 1-tablespoon (20g) sized balls. Roll them in the cinnamon-sugar mixture. Place them 2 inches apart on your prepared baking sheet. Bake for 8 to 10 minutes, until set around the edges. Let the cookies cool on the pan for 2 minutes, then transfer them to a wire rack to cool completely. Store at room temp in an airtight container for up to 4 days.

What a fun (and—for many of us—elusive!) feeling. While you're experiencing this beautiful lightness/have a juicy peach cobbler in the oven, let's spend some time focusing on life's simple pleasures. These pleasures look different for everyone, but mine include: eating something I grew in my garden, hearing my favorite song randomly playing on the radio, and not having to wait in line. There's no need to monitor yourself right now—it's 100 percent OK to take a break from the practical thoughts and tasks that come with being a human. Give yourself the space to truly savor this delicious feeling, without judgment.

peach cobbler

MAKES AN 8-INCH SQUARE COBBLER

Peach cobbler is one of those desserts that you can throw together in twenty minutes without a ton of concentration or dishes to wash. You don't even have to grease the pan—we're pouring melted butter directly in there, baby! It's also one of those desserts that almost everyone seems to enjoy. Have you ever been around a peach cobbler and someone was like, "No, I'm not really into peach cobbler"? Me neither.

My version combines sweet ripe peaches with the richness of brown butter, the tang of buttermilk, and the bright flavor of nutmeg. You'll end up with a yummy everyday dessert that your friends will certainly ask you to make whenever they come over for dinner.

½ cup (1 stick, 113g) unsalted butter

1½ cups (255g) fresh peaches sliced ¼ inch thick
   (from about 2 large peaches)

¼ cup (50g) light brown sugar

½ teaspoon ground cinnamon

⅛ teaspoon ground nutmeg

1 cup (130g) all-purpose flour

⅔ cup (133g) granulated sugar

1½ teaspoons baking powder

¼ teaspoon kosher salt

1 cup buttermilk

1 teaspoon vanilla extract

the how-to

1 Preheat the oven to 375°F and dig out your 8-inch square pan.

2 Brown your butter (see page 16). Pour it into the bottom of the pan.

3 In a medium bowl, stir together the peach slices, brown sugar, cinnamon, and nutmeg. Set aside until needed.

4 In a medium bowl, whisk together the flour, granulated sugar, baking powder, and salt. Add the buttermilk and vanilla extract and stir with a rubber spatula to combine.

5 Pour the batter into the pan over the butter and spread out into an even layer (but don't stir!). Evenly layer the peach mixture on top (pour any leftover juices over the top too).

6 Bake for 45 to 50 minutes, until the sides are bubbling and a tester inserted comes out clean. Let cool before slicing. Store in the fridge, covered, for up to 3 days.

note: You can leave the skin on the peaches— I hate having to peel things if I don't have to!

YOU MIGHT BE FEELING:
*preoccupied with feelings/
thoughts/memories of
another time/person*

I put nostalgia in the "happy" category, but I know it's a complex emotion that might feel different for you—in fact, it feels pretty complex to me. Sort of like a melancholic mix of longing and fondness, mixed with a desire to revisit or invoke particular feelings or moments from the past.

For some reason I experience nostalgia as a soft humming warmth in my upper stomach, creeping up my neck onto my cheeks. It sort of feels like that moment when you go too high on a swing and are suspended midair for a beat before you come back down. (Side note: If you haven't been on a swing lately, I recommend it.)

Nostalgia allows us to revisit both the good and the bad. Sometimes I'm nostalgic for the simple pleasures of Friday nights spent dancing with my friends and making out with people in cornfields. But sometimes I find myself feeling nostalgic for times that weren't particularly happy, or people who weren't particularly great for me. That can be really confusing. Try not to judge yourself for what you're feeling nostalgic about. Your experiences are yours to revisit, on your own terms.

egg yolk chocolate chip cookies

MAKES 13 COOKIES

For me, few things are more nostalgic than a chocolate chip cookie from my Midwestern grandma's kitchen. Especially if it's eaten right out of the oven, after snacking on cookie dough throughout the process. This recipe is different from my grandma's, but the feeling remains. Food is so tied to memory. When I take a bite of one of these, I can picture my six-year-old self sitting on the kitchen countertop helping to cream the butter and sugar and tossing in the chocolate chips.

These are chewy cookies with a crispy edge, and they're sprinkled with a healthy amount of flaky salt. The salt is there for aesthetic purposes of course (I mean, look at it), but it also heightens the other flavors on your tongue—dark brown sugar, vanilla, and semisweet chocolate. They're big, bakery-style cookies. We're using ¼ cup of dough for each! Yes, I said ¼ cup each!

2¼ cups (293g) all-purpose flour

1 teaspoon baking soda

½ teaspoon kosher salt

1 cup (2 sticks, 227g) room temp unsalted butter

¾ cup (150g) granulated sugar

½ cup (100g) dark brown sugar

1 large egg

2 large egg yolks

2 teaspoons vanilla extract

1½ cups (263g) semisweet chocolate chips

flaky salt (such as Maldon), for sprinkling

the how-to

1 Preheat the oven to 350°F and line a baking sheet with parchment paper.

2 In a medium bowl, whisk together the flour, baking soda, and salt.

3 In the bowl of a stand mixer fitted with the paddle attachment, beat the butter, granulated sugar, and brown sugar on medium-high speed until creamy, about 2 minutes. Beat in the egg, egg yolks, and vanilla extract. Add the flour mixture and mix on low speed. Stir in the chocolate chips, scraping the bottom of the bowl with the spatula to make sure everything's all mixed in.

4 Scoop into ¼-cup (80g) balls (I use a cookie scoop for this, but you can also use an ice cream scoop or super large spoon). Arrange on the prepared baking sheet at least 3 inches apart. Bake for 14 to 16 minutes, until golden all over and browned around the edges. Sprinkle with flaky salt. Let the cookies cool on the pan for 2 minutes, then transfer them to a wire rack to cool completely. Store at room temp in an airtight container for up to 2 days.

YOU MIGHT BE FEELING:

*a carefree youthful vibrance,
like you're able to exist
contently in the here and now*

I really love my inner child. Like, really love her. But that wasn't always true! I used to feel pretty disconnected from my younger self. Then one day, my therapist suggested I choose a picture of myself as a child that I like and print it out. I chose a picture of me in bright pink overalls standing in front of my prized garden flowers with a huge smile splashed across my face. I can feel the optimism, joy, and pride bursting through the picture. Adding a tool to actually visualize my younger self helped me access my inner child in a way that just talking about it couldn't. I still keep the photo up on my fridge.

Something that I love so much about children is their ability to be playful, without worrying about who is watching, or how it makes them look. They're able to go with the feeling completely. It's truly inspiring. And today, we're going to follow their lead by making a birthday-esque strawberry funfetti cake just because.

strawberry funfetti cake

MAKES AN 8-INCH SQUARE SINGLE-LAYER CAKE

Is it really a celebration without cake? Humor me: close your eyes and picture a celebration cake. OK, open them. You probably pictured a big deal three-layer type of cake designed with birthday parties in mind, right? OK, scratch that. Now I want you to imagine what it might be like to honor and celebrate your tiny joys. Like: you felt that first bite of chilly weather on your cheeks, or it's the anniversary of the day you went out for pizza and realized you were in love, or you finally got to meet your friend's new puppy, or you parallel parked in one try with cars behind you on a busy road on the left side. This recipe is designed for those *little* joys that are totally worth celebrating.

You'll wind up with a pretty in pink strawberry cake with swooshes of strawberry buttercream on top and tons of sprinkles throughout. Also, hopefully, a dose of playfulness.

FOR THE CAKE

¼ cup (15g) freeze-dried strawberries

1⅔ cups (216g) all-purpose flour

1 cup (200g) granulated sugar

1½ teaspoons baking powder

½ teaspoon kosher salt

2 large egg whites

½ cup whole milk

¼ cup (60g) sour cream

¼ cup (50g) melted coconut oil

2 teaspoons vanilla extract

¼ teaspoon almond extract

2 tablespoons rainbow sprinkles

¼ cup (15g) freeze-dried strawberries

½ cup (1 stick, 113g) room temp unsalted butter

1¼ cups (150g) powdered sugar

1 teaspoon vanilla extract

1 tablespoon whole milk

the how-to: cake

1   Preheat the oven to 350°F. Line the bottom and two sides of an 8-inch square pan with a length of parchment paper cut to the width of the bottom of the pan. Grease the parchment paper and two exposed sides of the pan.

2   In a food processor, grind the freeze-dried strawberries into a fine powder.

3   In a large bowl, whisk together the flour, granulated sugar, strawberry powder, baking powder, and salt. In a medium bowl, whisk together the egg whites, milk, sour cream, coconut oil, vanilla extract, and almond extract. Pour the dry ingredients into the wet ingredients and whisk until thoroughly combined. Gently fold in the sprinkles.

4   Bake for 30 to 35 minutes, until a tester inserted in the center comes out with moist crumbs. Let cool for 10 minutes in the pan, then turn out onto a wire rack to cool completely.

the how-to: frosting & assembly

1   In a food processor, grind the freeze-dried strawberries into a fine powder.

2   In the bowl of a stand mixer, beat the butter on medium speed until creamy, about 1 minute. Slowly add in the powdered sugar. Beat until light and fluffy, about 2 minutes. Add the strawberry powder, vanilla extract, and milk and beat to combine.

3   When the cake is completely cool, frost the top using an offset spatula. Decorate with additional sprinkles. Store at room temperature in an airtight container for up to 2 days.

There aren't enough opportunities to talk up and celebrate ourselves. On an ongoing basis, you handle things that scare you, figure things out that seem impossible, and build a beautiful life. Those things all deserve to be celebrated. But we're often discouraged from outwardly showing pride in ourselves, which can inflame some pretty unhelpful worries that we're being self-centered or conceited. This is bullshit! You are 100 percent allowed to cheer yourself on. There is no shame in celebrating your wins, and there's only self-love and self-confidence to gain. Take a minute and channel Reese Witherspoon at the end of *Legally Blonde*: "You must always have faith in people. And, most importantly, you must always have faith in yourself."

And if you're proud of someone else today, baking is always a great expression of your love and support.

salted peanut butter pie

MAKES A 9-INCH PIE

Imagine the Cool Whip–based, butter-crust peanut butter pie you've surely eaten at a diner at some point. Now let it go, because this pie is nothing like that! OK, it's a little like that, but the differences are important to note. A slice of this baby is a silky sweet/salty piece of yum. I'm not sure if this description helps or hurts my cause, but the texture of this graham cracker–crusted pie is just like a pumpkin pie—light and smooth at room temperature, thicker and creamy straight out of the fridge. Is it weird? A little. But I prefer the term *innovative*! If you're not convinced, there's also a chocolate drizzle.

This pie is meant to be shared and savored with your people. If you're proud of yourself today, tell someone about it! If you're proud of someone else, celebrate them!

FOR THE CRUST

1½ cups (150g) graham cracker crumbs
2 tablespoons light brown sugar
a tiny pinch of kosher salt
6 tablespoons (85g) melted unsalted butter

FOR THE FILLING

½ cup (100 grams) light brown sugar
2 large eggs
1 teaspoon vanilla extract
1¼ cups heavy cream
½ teaspoon kosher salt
¾ cup (165g) creamy peanut butter
    (not natural!)

2 tablespoons semisweet chocolate

1½ teaspoons heavy cream

flaky salt (such as Maldon), for sprinkling

the how-to: crust

1 Preheat the oven to 350°F.

2 In a medium bowl, combine the graham cracker crumbs, brown sugar, and salt. Stir in the melted butter. Press the crust firmly into the bottom and sides of a 9-inch pie plate (I find it helps to use the bottom of a measuring cup or glass).

3 Bake for 8 to 10 minutes, until lightly golden. Remove from the oven (leave the oven on) and set aside to cool for a few minutes.

the how-to: filling

1 In a large bowl, whisk together the brown sugar, eggs, vanilla extract, heavy cream, and salt. Add the peanut butter and whisk until totally smooth. Pour into the prepared pie crust.

2 Set the pie on a rimmed baking sheet and bake for 35 to 40 minutes, until the center looks set.

the how-to: topping

While the pie is baking, combine the chocolate and heavy cream in a small heatproof bowl. Microwave in 30-second increments, stirring in between, until smooth. Let cool slightly. Transfer to a piping bag or Ziploc bag (cut the end off before using).

the how-to: assembly

Remove the pie from the oven and let it cool on a wire rack for 20 minutes. Drizzle it with the chocolate and sprinkle it generously with flaky salt. Transfer to the fridge to cool completely, about 4 hours. Serve at room temperature or cold (I prefer cold!). Store in the fridge, covered, for up to 2 days.

note: To make the graham cracker crumbs, put whole graham crackers into a gallon-sized Ziploc bag and crush them with a rolling pin.

RELIEVED

～～～

YOU MIGHT BE FEELING:
*grateful that things fell
into place, like you can
take a full breath*

～～～

First: let out a big sigh of relief. I'm serious—breathe out audibly through your mouth and let your body relax in a dramatic stage acting kind of way. You've probably been carrying a lot of tension. What a truly great feeling it is to let it all out and remind yourself that sometimes things really do work out. I'm glad you're having a calm moment amid life's chaos. Now try to leave that space empty! There's no need to immediately start thinking about things you need to do or worry about. While you're making your cookies, maybe even try leaving your phone in the other room.

oatmeal cookies

MAKES ABOUT 18 COOKIES

If you're feeling relieved right now, that probably means you've been spending a lot of time and energy worrying about something. Luckily, there's nothing to worry about with an oatmeal cookie—it's a pretty basic recipe, and there's nothing wrong with that! Sometimes you just need something easy, that you know you'll like, and you know will turn out exactly how you want. That's when these babies come in!

They're the oatmeal cookie you know and love, but flavored with walnuts and orange zest. If you are like "Come on, I just want something easy, don't make me zest an orange," that's OK. This recipe would be delicious with oats only! But if you want the full relaxing oatmeal cookie experience, add the mix-ins. But not raisins. Never raisins!

1 cup (2 sticks, 227g) unsalted butter

1⅓ cups (173g) all-purpose flour

¾ teaspoon baking soda

1 teaspoon kosher salt

1 cup (200g) dark brown sugar

½ cup (100g) granulated sugar

1 teaspoon fresh orange zest

2 large eggs

1 large egg yolk

2 teaspoons vanilla extract

2½ cups (250g) old-fashioned rolled oats

½ cup (75g) toasted chopped walnuts

the how-to

1 Brown your butter (see page 16). Pour it into a heatproof bowl, cover, and refrigerate for 30 minutes (it will still be melted when you pull it out—we're just looking for not hot!).

2 In a medium bowl, whisk together the flour, baking soda, and salt.

3 In the bowl of a stand mixer fitted with the paddle attachment, cream together the butter, brown sugar, granulated sugar, and orange zest on medium-high speed for about 2 minutes (it won't look smooth). Scrape down the bowl. Add the eggs, egg yolk, and vanilla extract and beat on medium-high speed until light colored and smooth, about a minute more.

4 Add the flour mixture and mix on low speed until incorporated. Scrape down the bowl. Add the oats and walnuts and mix on low speed just until combined. Give it a good stir with a rubber spatula to make sure everything's evenly incorporated.

5 Refrigerate the dough for about 1 hour. While you're waiting, preheat the oven to 350°F and line a baking sheet with parchment paper.

6 Roll the dough into 3-tablespoon (60g) balls. Place them at least 3 inches apart on the baking sheet. Bake for 13 to 15 minutes, until set around the edges. Store at room temp in an airtight container for up to 3 days.

YOU MIGHT BE FEELING:
*like things worked out as they
should have, like the universe
has meaning, like you've
done something worthwhile*

We use the word *satisfying* to describe our feelings about food all the time. We use it to describe flavor, texture, and whether we've eaten our fill or not. I might argue it's the most tied-to-food feeling in this book. Strangely enough, I wrote about this feeling last, after I'd written everything else. I didn't mean to save it 'til the end (it just worked out that way) but it's kind of poetic, huh! Satisfaction is a close cousin of pride. So, if it's relevant here, take a second to reflect on one thing you did for yourself today or crossed off your list—even if it was just getting out of bed and brushing your teeth! It's so important to celebrate our own achievements and accomplishments, the same way we celebrate other people's. It's not frivolous or vain. You deserve it.

walnut & fig shortbread

MAKES ABOUT THIRTY 2½-INCH COOKIES

There is something incredibly satisfying about the way a knife cuts through chilled dough, which is what you'll do here to slice your cookies into rounds. Satisfaction comes in big and small forms. I suspect the reason you turned to this page might be due to the big kind (yay!), but here's a small one to pair with it.

Here, we've got a nutmeg-spiced shortbread cookie base with toasted walnuts and sweet chopped figs scattered throughout. Slice and bake cookies are the underrated heroes of bake sales and holiday parties. You can make the dough and keep it in your freezer until you need it, you don't have to scoop anything, and with your mix-ins— they're just *pretty*. I know they're not exactly exciting, but they absolutely get the job done well.

1 cup (2 sticks, 227g) room temp unsalted butter

⅔ cup (132g) light brown sugar

2 teaspoons vanilla extract

½ teaspoon kosher salt

a pinch of ground nutmeg

2¼ cups (293g) all-purpose flour

½ cup (75g) finely (but not *too* finely!) chopped toasted walnuts

½ cup (45g) finely (but not *too* finely!) chopped dried figs

¼ cup (50g) granulated sugar, for rolling

the how-to

1 In the bowl of a stand mixer fitted with the paddle attachment, cream together the butter and brown sugar on medium-high speed until light and fluffy, about 2 minutes. Beat in the vanilla extract, salt, and nutmeg. With the mixer running on low speed, add the flour and mix until the dough comes together. Pour in the walnuts and figs and mix until just combined. Scrape the bottom of the bowl with a spatula to make sure everything's mixed in.

2 Divide the dough into two and roll each half into a 2-inch-wide log. Wrap each log in plastic wrap—you can use the plastic wrap to help even out the log! Refrigerate for 1 hour, or if you're in a hurry, freeze for 30 minutes.

3 Preheat the oven to 325°F and line a baking sheet with parchment paper.

4 Using a sharp knife, cut each dough log into ¼-inch rounds. Roll the edges of each cookie into the granulated sugar.

5 Place the cookies 2 inches apart on the baking sheet. Bake for 15 to 17 minutes, until the center of the cookies look set. Let the cookies cool on the pan for 2 minutes, then transfer them to a wire rack. Store at room temp in an airtight container for up to a week.

~~~~~~~~

like you're in elementary school on field day and you got to throw water balloons with your friends

~~~~~~~~

Maybe at this moment you feel very much like yourself. I love silliness because it temporarily suspends some pretty rigid social rules of adulthood that prevent us from fully enjoying, or even fully feeling. Feel free to take up space here—silliness gives us room to breathe!

Silliness allows us to explore without concern about what people might think. It provides a well-deserved break from the burden of expectations and responsibility. It's also one of my favorite ways to connect with my friends. Being silly *together* is an incredible way to grow closer to people (adults and children alike) and strengthen your bond. Bonus: it feels really good. Take a second and think of a time that you were totally overtaken by contagious laughter with your friend(s). Now do me a favor: jot the thought down now, then mail the aforementioned friend a postcard unannounced that says "Remember that time that . . . [your story here]." Bonus if you don't sign it.

orange creamsicle cake

MAKES A 9-INCH 2-LAYER CAKE

I've paired this recipe with silliness because it's so deeply connected to memories of chasing down the ice cream truck as a child. In my case, the chasing was usually post-swim at the neighborhood pool—flip-flops slapping against the pavement and soaking wet towel streaming behind. You might not have this same very specific memory, but you likely have eaten a creamsicle: vanilla ice cream swirled with tangy orange sherbet iciness. When I take a bite of this cake, I can almost feel the pool water on my skin.

The two-layer cake is lightly vanilla-orange flavored—no orange extract here, just fresh zest and juice! The frosting is a German buttercream, which is basically custard (my fave) whipped up with a bunch of butter into a light, fluffy, and not overly sweet cloud. It's the slightly fussier cousin of Swiss buttercream.

FOR THE CAKE

1 tablespoon fresh orange zest

2 cups (400g) granulated sugar

3 cups (390g) cake flour

1 tablespoon baking powder

1 teaspoon kosher salt

¾ cup freshly squeezed orange juice

½ cup heavy cream

2 teaspoons vanilla extract

½ cup vegetable oil

4 large egg whites

¾ cup (150g) granulated sugar

⅓ cup (37g) cornstarch

1 teaspoon fresh orange zest

scant ¼ teaspoon kosher salt

2 large eggs

1 cup whole milk

1 tablespoon vanilla extract

1½ cups (3 sticks, 340g) room temp
  unsalted butter

the how-to: cake

1　Preheat the oven to 350°F. Line the bottoms of two 9-inch round cake pans with parchment paper. Grease the pans and parchment paper.

2　In a medium bowl, rub the orange zest into the granulated sugar (this will help release more flavor from the zest!). Add the cake flour, baking powder, and salt and whisk until combined.

3　In a glass measuring cup or small bowl, stir together the orange juice, heavy cream, and vanilla extract.

4　In a large bowl, whisk together the vegetable oil and egg whites. Add the flour mixture and orange juice mixture in two alternating batches, whisking between each addition.

5　Bake for 20 to 25 minutes, until a tester inserted in the middle comes out with moist crumbs. Cool for 10 minutes in the pan, then turn the layers out onto wire racks to cool completely.

the how-to: buttercream & assembly

1　In a medium saucepan (don't turn on the stove yet!), whisk together the granulated sugar, cornstarch, orange zest, and salt. Add the eggs one at a time, whisking thoroughly between each addition. Slowly pour in the milk, whisking constantly. Turn on the heat to medium and whisk constantly until the mixture starts to bubble. Once bubbling, continue whisking for 1 minute, or until very thick. Remove it from the heat and whisk in the vanilla extract. Scrape the custard into the bowl of your electric mixer and put it in the fridge to cool completely, about 30 minutes.

2　Once cool, beat the custard in your stand mixer using the whisk attachment on medium-high speed for 2 minutes. With the machine running, add the butter a couple of tablespoons at a time. Continue whipping on medium-high speed for about 4 minutes, until very, very fluffy.

3　Using an offset spatula, fill and frost the cake! For this one, I usually fill the middle and frost the top with thick layers and coat the sides with just a very thin layer, naked cake style. Store in an airtight container at room temperature for up to 3 days.

note: You'll need about 4 large oranges to get enough freshly squeezed juice for this recipe!

OK, first of all: How do you feel about surprises? Choose one:

I love being surprised!!!

Why would I want to be surprised when I could be prepared?

This topic can be pretty polarizing—people tend to have strong feelings about surprises. Those feelings might also depend on the context. For instance: I wouldn't want to know about my surprise birthday party, but I do want to know what happens at the end of the movie before I start watching it. I shelved "surprise" in "happy," but it's absolutely OK if you're experiencing a not-so-happy surprise today. A pie is helpful either way.

apple crumb pie

MAKES A 9-INCH PIE

I'm a proud two-time winner of the Adams Morgan neighborhood apple pie contest (I have the certificate displayed prominently in my home), so I'll admit to having a particular affection for apple pie, as well as strong opinions about it.

For example: I believe apple pies are best with a crumble topping—not a double crust. I'm not sure if I've told you this, but I'm relatively anti–double crust. Yes, they are very beautiful. But I think they take away from the real showstopper: the filling! We're using green apples for this recipe because I love their tartness and their texture when baked down. We're adding the usual suspects: brown sugar, cinnamon, cloves, and nutmeg. We're also adding brown butter and a couple of tablespoons of bourbon for flavor.

Back to the apple pie contest—I paired this particular recipe with this particular emotion because of my intense joy at the surprise of being announced the winner. It was for sure the biggest celebrity moment of my life.

FOR THE CRUST

1 recipe Single Pie crust (page 238)

FOR THE CRUMBLE

¾ cup (98g) all-purpose flour
⅔ cup (133g) light brown sugar
a pinch of kosher salt
6 tablespoons (85g) melted unsalted butter

4 tablespoons (½ stick, 57g) unsalted butter

4 large green apples

½ cup (100g) light brown sugar

½ teaspoon ground cinnamon

⅛ teaspoon ground cloves

a pinch of ground nutmeg

½ teaspoon kosher salt

2 tablespoons bourbon

3 tablespoons tapioca starch

the how-to: crust

1 Preheat the oven to 350°F.

2 Roll out your pie crust to an 11-inch circle. Transfer the dough to a 9-inch pie plate. Fold the excess under so the edge of the crust lines up with the edge of the pie plate. Crimp the edge decoratively. Pop the crust into the freezer until needed.

the how-to: crumble

In a small bowl, stir together all the crumb topping ingredients with a fork until crumbs form—the largest pieces should be the size of kidney beans. Set aside in the fridge until needed.

the how-to: filling

1 Brown your butter (see page 16), then set it aside to cool slightly.

2 Peel the apples, halve them starting at the stem, then slice each half lengthwise into ¼-inch-thick slices.

3 In a large bowl, stir together the apples, brown sugar, cinnamon, cloves, nutmeg, salt, bourbon, and brown butter with a rubber spatula. Add the tapioca starch and stir thoroughly to combine.

4 Transfer the apple mixture into your prepared pie crust and pour any remaining juices over the top. Sprinkle the crumb topping evenly on top of the apples.

5 Bake for 1 hour, or until the juices are bubbling up through the crumb topping and the crust is deeply golden brown. Let sit on a wire rack for at least 3 hours (I know, I know) to allow the pie to thicken completely before serving. If you want warm apple pie, heat it up in the microwave later! Store at room temp in an airtight container for up to 2 days.

note: If your crust or crumble is browning too quickly, put a piece of foil over it! It's easy: turn a large mixing bowl upside down, form the foil around it, and then tent it over your pie.

sad

The recipes in this chapter are here to keep you company when you're going through it.

Vibes: Gloomy gray skies, Adele's song "Someone Like You" on repeat

Before we get started, let's be clear about something: you don't owe anyone happiness or positivity. There is a deeply entrenched, culturally reinforced fear of feeling or expressing sadness in our society, which isn't exactly healthy or realistic, but it is understandable. After all, feeling our pain can be, well, painful. It takes a lot of strength and vulnerability to allow yourself to be sad. Sitting with sad feelings—yours, or another person's—is uncomfortable. Sometimes, in an attempt to avoid engaging with these tough feelings, we kick into high gear trying to *solve the problem*. It can be helpful to stop and ask yourself: Am I actually trying to solve the problem or am I trying not to experience sadness?

Of course, sometimes we don't really know why we're sad. Sometimes we might just feel like a nebulous dark cloud is floating around us. So here I want to invite you to give yourself permission to explore the "why." We have a tendency to discount our feelings if we think they don't meet the threshold for what "counts" as a sad event. Maybe your favorite coffee shop had to close down in the midst of the COVID pandemic. Maybe you detected a strange tone (that may or may not actually be there!) in your partner's voice. Maybe your kid is having a rough time at school this year. Maybe your best friend recently moved. Maybe you didn't get the promotion you know you deserve. Your feelings are valid, regardless of the cause you trace them back to. Do me a favor? Take a break from the self-judgment, at the very least until you pull your cake/cookies/pie/etc. out of the oven.

Sometimes life is really hard. Sometimes life is really hard for a really long time. Sometimes it's hard to care for yourself—maybe you're finding it difficult right now to brush your teeth, feed yourself dinner, or pick your clothes up off the floor. There's absolutely no need to beat yourself up over any of that. You are making it through the day, and that is more than enough.

Sadness can be a lonely place. Often, it seems like it's easier to share our happiness than our sadness. Maybe you don't want to burden anyone, or maybe you aren't sure how to explain what you're feeling in a way that you think will make sense, or maybe the sadness just feels too deep and remote. But even if you believe that no one will understand your particular situation (and it's true that we all live unique lives), that doesn't mean that people can't show up for you and care for you. You don't have to carry everything, I promise. Let's invite someone over for tea and a slice of cake, OK?

sad

awkward

discouraged

bored

gloomy

doubtful

frazzled

homesick

heartbroken

inadequate

hopeless

jealous

lonely

rejected

pessimistic

sorrowful

sad

YOU MIGHT BE FEELING:
*a desire to be someone or
somewhere else—anyone
and anywhere else*

There are many variations of awkward, and none of them are very comfortable to experience. But for me, feeling awkward is almost always a by-product of unrealistic expectations I've set for myself, or some incorrect perceptions other people have set on me. I expect that I should know what to say in every instance, I should always be able to accurately read tone/meaning/intent, and I should never make any social miscalculations. But that's impossible, of course. And a lot of times, something that feels unbearably awkward to me is something that people around me don't even notice.

And even if they do, it's so, so fleeting. If it helps you, please know that I don't even remember what I had for breakfast yesterday, so that one guy who works at your favorite pizza spot definitely doesn't remember the time he brought your pizza to the table and told you to enjoy your meal and you accidentally said "You too." Existing in the world and communicating with other people is inherently messy, and messiness is totally fine.

You are soooo not alone in this feeling.

kitchen sink cookies

MAKES ABOUT 24 COOKIES

These chewy, lumpy cookies are the dessert embodiment of awkwardness. They're made up of a little bit of everything, an assortment of flavors and textures that you might not expect to hang well together—but this cookie is greater than the sum of its parts. Sometimes you just need the novelty of a treat with a lot going on, and these do the job.

Other/alternative mix-ins include (but are not limited to): M&M's, pretzels, dried fruit (not my vibe, but you do you), other kinds of chopped nuts, various kinds of cereal, crushed potato chips.

2 cups (260g) all-purpose flour

1 teaspoon baking soda

½ teaspoon kosher salt

1 teaspoon espresso powder

1 cup (2 sticks, 227g) room temp unsalted butter

⅔ cup (133g) light brown sugar

¼ cup (50g) granulated sugar

1 large egg

1 teaspoon vanilla extract

¾ cup (21g) crushed cornflakes

½ cup (75g) toasted and chopped pecans

¾ cup (131g) milk chocolate chips

½ cup (56g) sweetened coconut flakes

flaky salt (such as Maldon), for sprinkling (optional)

the how-to

1 Preheat the oven to 325°F and line a baking sheet with parchment paper.

2 In a medium bowl, whisk together the flour, baking soda, salt, and espresso powder.

3 In the bowl of a stand mixer, cream together the butter and sugars on medium-high speed until light and fluffy, about 2 minutes. Beat in the egg and vanilla extract. Mix in the flour mixture on low speed. Add the cornflakes, pecans, chocolate chips, and coconut flakes and mix on low speed until just incorporated. Scoop into 2-tablespoon (40g) balls, arrange 2 inches apart on the cookie sheet, and sprinkle with flaky salt, if desired. If you're feeling *particular* today, press some toppings into the tops of your dough balls after you roll 'em—that way they'll show up on the top (thank you to the brilliant food stylist Olivia Caminiti for this tip)!

4 Bake for 13 to 15 minutes, until the edges of the cookies are lightly golden. Let cool for 2 minutes, then transfer to a wire rack. Store at room temp in an airtight container for up to 2 days.

~

YOU MIGHT BE FEELING:
*like you should be doing
something else but who knows
what that thing actually is*

~

If you're bored, you've come to the right book! Good job for putting that restless energy toward creating. But first, I do want to note that you don't constantly have to be doing something. It's OK to rest, really. We live under the bleak expectation that our value is tied to our output, and that we must constantly produce things. Even when you recognize that standard isn't fair, it can still be very difficult to shake the feeling that you should be *doing* something.

Baking isn't always a form of rest—I see you hammering out those cookies for that bake sale, churning out muffins for your in-laws' impending overnight visit. But if you're saying, "No, Becca, I'm actually just bored and really want something to do"—proceed. Let's see if we can just get into the groove of making something for enjoyment. Our ultimate goal here is to become fixated on and immersed in the *process* rather than the outcome. Because truly, if you focus on the process, the outcome tends to turn out well anyway. Yeasted doughs are perfect for this because they force you to slow down and pay attention to what you're creating. Not to mention it's practically magic—the dough rises before your very eyes! This is truly the "baking by feel" part.

coffee-glazed cinnamon rolls

MAKES 12 ROLLS

I'm going to be honest: I don't really like cinnamon rolls. But I love these. They're a sweet and fluffy pastry swirled with a deep/warm/cinnamon-y filling, finished off with a rich coffee glaze. They will make your house smell amazing. Everyone will ask you to make them again.

This is a hands-on recipe, so let's try really engaging with our senses. Focus on the grainy texture of the cinnamon-sugar mixture when you're sprinkling it, the soft and springy texture of the dough when you're rolling it up into a cylinder, and the silky texture of the icing when you're drizzling it over the warm rolls.

You'll need a somewhat odd tool for this recipe: dental floss! Unflavored is best, but mint is fine. Why floss, you might ask? We want to avoid using a knife to cut our rolls because it'll squash our dough.

FOR THE DOUGH

1 cup whole milk
½ cup (1 stick, 113g) unsalted butter, cut into ½-inch slices
4½ cups (585g) all-purpose flour + more if needed
¼ cup (50g) granulated sugar
¼ cup (50g) light brown sugar
2¼ teaspoons (7g, 1 standard packet) active dry yeast
1 teaspoon kosher salt
2 large eggs
a couple teaspoons of vegetable oil, to coat the bowl

1 cup (200g) light brown sugar

2 tablespoons ground cinnamon

¼ teaspoon ground nutmeg

¼ teaspoon kosher salt

4 tablespoons (½ stick, 57g) softened unsalted
   butter

6 tablespoons (85g) softened unsalted butter

4 oz (113g) softened cream cheese

2 cups (240g) powdered sugar

1 teaspoon espresso powder

a pinch of kosher salt

3 tablespoons strongly brewed coffee, cooled

the how-to: rolls

1   In a glass measuring cup (or medium heatproof bowl), combine the milk and butter. Microwave in 30-second increments, stirring in between, until the butter is just melted. Set aside to cool to lukewarm temperature.

2   In the bowl of a stand mixer fitted with the dough hook attachment, combine the flour, granulated sugar, brown sugar, yeast, and salt.

3   Add the eggs to the lukewarm milk/butter mixture and whisk with a fork to combine. Pour the wet ingredient mixture into the dry ingredient mixture. Knead the mixture with the dough hook for 7 to 9 minutes, until it feels slightly sticky but smooth. If your dough feels too wet, add another tablespoon or two of flour. Scrape the dough out onto a lightly floured surface and lightly coat the bowl in vegetable oil. Return the dough to the bowl and cover

it with plastic wrap. Let rise out on the counter for 1½ to 2 hours (depending on how warm your kitchen is), until nearly doubled in size.

the how-to: filling

1   While the dough is rising, make your filling. In a medium bowl, whisk together the brown sugar, cinnamon, nutmeg, and salt. Make sure your butter is softened and ready to go.

2   Once the dough has risen, turn it out onto a lightly floured surface. Roll it out into a 12 x 18-inch rectangle. Coat the rectangle evenly with the softened butter. Scatter the filling mixture evenly over the top. Starting on a long edge, roll the dough up into a tight cylinder. Pinch the seam to seal. Using dental floss, cut the cylinder into 12 equal sections. I do this by dividing it in half, dividing the two sections in half, and then dividing the four sections into three. A note on how to use the floss: holding the ends of the floss in opposite hands, slide the floss under the cylinder, then loop the two ends up and around the top of the dough round so the strings cross each other and pull the ends in opposite directions until the dough divides into two sections. If after reading this you're still like *Becca, what the fuck are you talking about*, there are YouTube videos about it!

3   Place each bun into a 9 x 13-inch pan— you'll end up with four rows of three. There will likely be a bit of space in between, but it's OK if they touch. Cover the pan with plastic wrap and set out on the counter to rise for another hour. While the buns are rising, preheat the oven to 350°F.

4   Bake for 30 to 33 minutes, until lightly golden brown on the top.

the how-to: frosting & assembly

1   While the buns are in the oven, make your frosting! In the bowl of a stand mixer fitted with the paddle attachment, beat the butter and cream cheese on medium-high speed until smooth, about 1 minute. Add the powdered sugar, espresso powder, and salt and beat until creamy, about another minute. Add the coffee and beat until combined.

2   As soon as you take the buns out of the oven, pour the glaze over them and spread it around evenly. I highly, highly recommend eating these while they're warm from the oven. Whatever's left you can store in the fridge, covered, for up to 5 days. Reheat in the microwave!

note: If you want to make this an overnight recipe, put the plastic wrap–covered pan of cut buns into the fridge and leave overnight. In the morning, put them out on the counter and leave for 1 to 1½ hours, until they look puffy, then proceed to the baking.

DISCOURAGED

~~~~~~

YOU MIGHT BE FEELING:
*like crawling under your covers
and staying there indefinitely*

~~~~~~

Today you might be feeling like the world is too much and you're not enough. Since there are lots of potential sources for feeling discouraged, it's an easy trap to fall into. You could be discouraged about what's going on in the world, what's happening at your job, or the state of your relationship with someone you love. Regardless, it's absolutely OK to have days when you're not feeling particularly optimistic.

Real quick, turn to "lighthearted" on page 50. If you've made the peach cobbler, you should have a list of reasons you are wonderful and reasons life in general is wonderful all ready to go. Take a minute to read them. Try to remember that these things are still true, even if you're having trouble seeing them today. Try to remember that the way you're feeling right now isn't permanent.

And if you haven't filled out the lists yet, text your best friend(s) and say "Hey, what's your fave thing about me?" I'm absolutely positive they'd be more than happy to tell you.

pineapple spice cake

MAKES A STANDARD LOAF CAKE

This loaf cake is my version of a pineapple upside-down cake (minus the maraschino cherries—because, I mean, who really needs those?). The top, or bottom—depending on timing—layer is made up of juicy pineapple covered in a sticky caramel-like brown sugar mixture spiked with warming spices. The rest is a standard vanilla pound cake—which, let me say, is *not* a boring cake.

The main event of this recipe is flipping the cake over to get it out of the pan. It does take some faith in the process. But I'm always amazed at how, with some patience, it eventually drops right out. The result is a beautiful/shiny/magnificent fruit-topped hunk of dessert. It's hard to remain in a rut of discouragement when you create something as aesthetically appealing (and delicious) as an upside-down cake.

FOR THE TOPPING

4 tablespoons (½ stick, 57g) melted unsalted butter

½ cup (100g) dark brown sugar

½ teaspoon ground cinnamon

¼ teaspoon ground cardamom

⅛ teaspoon ground nutmeg

5 fresh or canned pineapple rings,
    sliced ¼ inch thick and halved

1¾ cups (228g) all-purpose flour

½ teaspoon baking powder

½ teaspoon kosher salt

1 cup (2 sticks, 227g) room temp unsalted butter

1¼ cups (250g) granulated sugar

3 large eggs

3 large egg yolks

1 tablespoon vanilla extract

½ cup (120g) sour cream

the how-to: topping

1   Preheat the oven to 350°F and grease a 9 x 5-inch loaf pan (not an 8 x 4-inch! It will overflow!).

2   In a small bowl, stir together the melted butter, brown sugar, cinnamon, cardamom, and nutmeg until smooth. Spread the mixture evenly in the bottom of your loaf pan. Arrange the pineapple slices in three rows on top of the butter mixture.

the how-to: cake

1   In a medium bowl, whisk together the flour, baking powder, and salt. In the bowl of a stand mixer, cream together the butter and granulated sugar on medium-high speed until light and fluffy, about 3 minutes. Scrape down the sides of the bowl. With the mixer running, add in the eggs and egg yolks one at a time, beating thoroughly between each one. Beat in the vanilla extract.

2   Add the flour mixture and sour cream in two alternating batches, starting and ending with the flour mixture. Mix on low speed just until combined. Spoon the batter into your prepared loaf pan and spread it evenly. Tap the pan on the counter a couple of times to get rid of any air bubbles.

3   Bake for 60 to 70 minutes, until a tester inserted in the center comes out with moist crumbs.

4   Let the cake cool for 10 minutes in the pan, then turn it out onto a wire rack, leaving the pan on top of the cake. Wait 30 seconds, then lift the pan off. Let cool completely. Serve with ice cream! Store at room temp in an airtight container for up to 3 days.

YOU MIGHT BE FEELING:
*a lack of trust in yourself,
others, institutions, or situations*

I think of this feeling as the patron saint of imposter syndrome. Doubting yourself is extremely common, but it's important to remember that the doubts you have about yourself are not facts—they just take up a lot of mental space. When you're full of doubt, there's less room for your hopes, dreams, ideas, and passions.

But maybe today you're not doubting *yourself*: maybe you're doubting a relationship, situation, or institution. I want to honor your perception! If you have a gut feeling that something isn't right, you are under absolutely no obligation to convince yourself otherwise.

I suppose the overall point I'm getting at here is about trusting yourself—your experience, expertise, and intuition. You're the expert on yourself, no need to doubt that!

blueberry pancake cake

MAKES AN 8-INCH TWO-LAYER CAKE

I know that sometimes people are hesitant about disrupting the balance of the universe by trying to reinvent a beloved food. I get it. But in this case, just trust me. You'll be making a tender two-layer cake flavored with the warm coziness of maple extract, filled and frosted with a rich and fluffy blueberry buttercream + some bonus blueberry preserves in the middle. It tastes exactly like blueberry pancakes (and yes, you can definitely eat it for breakfast).

Sometimes you ruin your best ideas before they even start by doubting yourself. And I'll admit: the first time I baked this cake, it didn't quite live up to my expectations texture-wise. In fact, it fell apart. But I decided not to listen to that annoying self-doubt and keep trying. I'm so glad I did.

FOR THE CAKE

2¼ cups (293g) all-purpose flour

2 teaspoons baking powder

1 teaspoon kosher salt

1 cup (2 sticks, 227g) room temp unsalted butter

¾ cup (150g) granulated sugar

½ cup (100g) light brown sugar

2 large eggs

1 teaspoon maple extract

1½ cups whole milk

1 cup (2 sticks, 227g) unsalted butter

4 cups (480g) powdered sugar

¼ cup (70g) blueberry preserves

1 teaspoon vanilla extract

a tiny pinch of kosher salt

½ (140g) cup blueberry preserves

the how-to: cake

1 Preheat the oven to 350°F and line the bottom of two 8-inch round cake pans with parchment paper. Grease the parchment paper and sides of the pan.

2 In a medium bowl, whisk together the flour, baking powder, and salt.

3 In the bowl of a stand mixer, cream together the butter, granulated sugar, and brown sugar on medium-high speed until light and fluffy, about 3 minutes. Beat in the eggs on medium-high speed, one at a time, until thoroughly combined. Scrape down the bottom and sides of the bowl. Add the maple extract. With the mixer running on low, add in the flour mixture and milk mixture in two alternating batches, starting and ending with the flour mixture. Scrape down the bottom and sides of the bowl one more time.

4 Spread the batter evenly into your prepared pans and smooth the tops.

5 Bake for 28 to 30 minutes, until the layers are golden brown and a tester inserted in the center comes out clean. Set on a wire rack to cool completely.

the how-to: frosting & assembly

1 In the bowl of a stand mixer, beat the butter on medium-high speed until creamy, about 2 minutes. With the mixer running on low, slowly add in the powdered sugar. Increase the speed to medium-high and beat until very fluffy, about 3 minutes. Beat in the blueberry preserves, vanilla, and salt.

2 Add a plop of frosting to the top of the first cake layer and, using an offset spatula, spread it out into an even layer about ½ inch thick. Add ⅓ cup of the buttercream into a piping bag or Ziploc bag and cut a ½-inch opening. Pipe a ring of frosting around the edge of the cake—this will keep your filling inside the cake! Fill in the center with the blueberry preserves. Stack the second layer on top. Frost the sides and top of the cake. Store in an airtight container in the fridge for up to 4 days.

FRAZZLED

~~~~~

YOU MIGHT BE FEELING:
pulled in too many directions,
full of anxious energy

~~~~~

You probably have a lot on your plate right now. So first, I want to remind you that you're doing a great job.

It might feel really difficult to devote any resources to your well-being right now. I know that when I'm feeling frazzled, it's hard to imagine doing one more thing—even if that thing will benefit me. So I invite you to try to frame this recipe not as a "task" to accomplish, but as simply an activity to take part in. And it doesn't have to have any particular outcome. If you want to make the dough and freeze it for your future self, that's fine. If you want to bake off these cookies and share them with your household, that's fine. If you want to just eat the dough by yourself, that's fine too.

The idea here is to engage in a low-stakes activity to slow down your mind and relieve some of the pressure from your day.

pecan & chocolate sandies

MAKES ABOUT THIRTY 2½-INCH COOKIES

When I did gymnastics as a kid, I used to finish out most practices with a packet of pecan sandies from the YMCA concessions stand. I can't tell you why exactly, since Oreos were also an option, and I will choose Oreos over any other packaged cookie pretty much every time. I suppose it just became a part of the routine. I ate those pecan sandies so many times that I can still taste the crumbly nuttiness and hear the crinkle of the packaging. But back to this recipe . . .

When you're spinning out in all directions, working with cookie dough is a nice way to ground yourself in the here and now. These straightforward, comforting, slice-and-bake cookies are designed to come together with minimal effort. If you're feeling frazzled, no problem. Just spend the next fifteenish minutes throwing together the ingredients, pop the dough in the fridge, eat a Popsicle or something, take the dough out of the fridge, slice, and bake. No need to make sure these are perfectly shaped, or perfectly uniform, or perfectly baked. They will be delicious in any form: a bit underdone or a bit over, perfectly round or a bit oblong.

FOR THE COOKIE DOUGH

1 cup (2 sticks, 227g) room temp unsalted butter
½ cup (100g) dark brown sugar
2 teaspoons vanilla extract

½ teaspoon kosher salt

2¼ cups (293g) all-purpose flour

½ cup (75g) finely chopped toasted pecans

½ cup (70g) finely chopped semisweet chocolate

FOR THE TOPPING

½ cup (70g) granulated sugar, for rolling

the how-to

1 In the bowl of a stand mixer, cream together the butter and brown sugar on medium-high speed until light and fluffy, about 2 minutes. Beat in the vanilla extract and salt. With the mixer running on low speed, add the flour and mix until the dough comes together. Pour in the pecans and chopped chocolate and mix until just combined. Scrape the bottom of the bowl with a spatula to make sure everything's mixed in!

2 Divide the dough into two and roll each half into a 2-inch-wide log. Wrap each log in plastic wrap—you can use the plastic wrap to help even out the log! Refrigerate for 1 hour, or if you're in a hurry, freeze for 30 minutes.

3 Preheat the oven to 325°F and line a baking sheet with parchment paper.

4 Using a sharp knife, cut each dough log into ½-inch rounds. Dip each cookie into the granulated sugar, lightly covering the entire surface.

5 Place the cookies 2 inches apart on the baking sheet. Bake for 16 to 18 minutes, until the centers are set. Let the cookies cool on the sheet for 2 minutes, then transfer them to a wire rack. Store at room temp in an airtight container for up to a week.

YOU MIGHT BE FEELING:
*like there's an ominous gray
cloud suspended threateningly
above your head specifically*

I'm strangely fond of gloominess. As an Enneagram 4, I think I even tend to romanticize it! Sometimes I'll purposely do things that pull me further into the gloom, like: listen to all the songs that bring up that particular brand of darkness (shout-out to Lucy Dacus's "Night Shift"), ruminate on past conversations/situations that I'm not happy with, or watch *Steel Magnolias* for the hundredth time.

All of this is to say, if you're feeling gloomy, I get it. But today, instead of just feeding it, maybe you can explore where that nebulous gloominess is coming from. Can you tie it to anything in particular?

I think of gloominess as one of those feelings that's almost always paired with other ones. So, are you also feeling lonely? Overwhelmed? Exhausted? Abandoned? Take a second to identify what some of these connected emotions might be.

ginger pudding pie

MAKES A 9-INCH PIE

I think you're going to like this recipe in part because it doesn't require making an actual, traditional pie crust. We're using graham cracker crumbs to significantly reduce the amount of effort we have to put in, and baby, it's beautiful. We're also going to make homemade pudding, and it's going to be fine. The flavors of this pie are basically the opposite of gloomy. We've got butter, we've got ginger, we've got maple, we've got cinnamon. Ultimately, they combine into a smooth and silky pudding on a rich graham cracker base, topped with a swoosh of whipped cream.

If this is your first time making pudding, I want to let you know that I *love* the moment when pudding suddenly, finally, thickens. This magical alchemy transforms a liquid that seemed like it might forever stay a watery mess into a divinely textured treat. Try letting yourself enjoy this simple trick—you can go back to feeling gloomy afterward if you want to, I promise.

FOR THE CRUST

1¼ cups (125g) graham cracker crumbs
2 tablespoons (25g) granulated sugar
6 tablespoons (85g) melted unsalted butter

FOR THE FILLING

¼ cup (35g) cornstarch
½ cup (100g) granulated sugar
2 teaspoons ground ginger
1 teaspoon ground cinnamon

¼ teaspoon kosher salt

2⅔ cups whole milk, divided

1 large egg

2 teaspoons vanilla extract

½ cup cold heavy cream

1 teaspoon honey

⅛ teaspoon maple extract

the how-to: crust

1 Preheat the oven to 350°F.

2 In a medium bowl, combine the graham cracker crumbs, granulated sugar, and melted butter. Press the crust firmly into the bottom and sides of the pie plate (I find it helps to use the bottom of a measuring cup or glass).

3 Bake for 12 to 14 minutes, until lightly golden. Remove the crust from the oven and set it aside to cool slightly. Turn off the oven—you won't need it anymore!

the how-to: filling

1 In a medium heatproof bowl, whisk together the cornstarch, granulated sugar, ground ginger, cinnamon, and salt. Gradually whisk in ⅔ cup of the milk, then the egg. In a heavy medium saucepan, bring the remaining 2 cups of milk to a gentle simmer over medium-low heat. Once the milk is simmering, turn off the heat. Carefully remove 1 cup of the hot milk and slowly pour it into the cornstarch mixture, whisking constantly. Pour the cornstarch mixture back into the saucepan over medium heat and whisk until bubbling. Whisk constantly for 2 minutes, or until the mixture thickens. Remove the pudding from the heat, then stir in the vanilla extract.

2 Pour the filling into the pie crust and refrigerate for at least 3 hours (you should chill too—watch a movie, or something).

the how-to: maple whipped cream & assembly

1 When you're almost ready to serve, start the whipped cream. In the bowl of a stand mixer fitted with the whisk attachment, beat the heavy cream, honey, and maple extract on medium-high speed until soft peaks form, about 3 minutes.

2 Plop the whipped cream on top of the pie and spread it out into an even layer using an offset spatula. Store in the fridge, covered, for up to 2 days.

HEARTBROKEN

〜〜〜

YOU MIGHT BE FEELING:
*a deep sense of sadness mixed
with abandonment or regret*

〜〜〜

I don't know about you, but for me this might be the most uncomfortable feeling in the entire book! Heartbreak makes me lose my appetite. I find that absolutely nothing tastes good, and food becomes a chore rather than a pleasure. I feel a truly unpleasant sinking ache in my chest that I might describe as dread. You might also have a sense of turning inward as an attempt to protect yourself from the raw vulnerability of opening your heart, just to have it squashed/broken/shrunken/shattered.

I want to let you know that there's absolutely no shame in showing that you're struggling. You don't benefit from hiding your pain and trying to manage it alone. There's no shame in mourning the loss of a relationship. It doesn't make you weak. It shows your beautiful capacity to love.

And now, we're going to wrap you in some sugar-coated love, with something that'll tempt those reluctant taste buds and hopefully offer you a bit of comfort. Bonus points if you invite a friend to join you and give you a much-needed hug!

peach bourbon cake

MAKES A 9-INCH SINGLE-LAYER CAKE

This recipe combines two of my favorite things: peaches and bourbon. It's low effort, high reward, and worth going to the store for. If you're heartbroken today, you need as much comfort as possible. You might also need something to take your mind off your racing, unhelpful thoughts. Enter, this cake. There's just something about single-layer cakes that feels so delightfully *manageable*. And it's an upside-down cake! So, it feels fancy.

I want you to make this cake in your pajamas. Yes, go put on your pajamas if you're not wearing them already. I don't care what time of day it is. Wearing your pajamas is fine. We're doing this because I don't really believe in wearing uncomfortable outside clothes inside the house, generally, but I *really* don't believe in wearing uncomfortable outside clothes inside the house when your heart is breaking. Life is just too short for that.

FOR THE PEACH LAYER

4 tablespoons (½ stick, 57g) melted unsalted butter
½ cup (100g) light brown sugar
1½ cups (255g) fresh peaches sliced ¼ inch thick, from about 2 medium peaches

1⅔ cups (216g) all-purpose flour

1½ teaspoons baking powder

½ teaspoon kosher salt

3 tablespoons bourbon

1½ teaspoons vanilla extract

½ cup room temp whole milk

½ cup (1 stick, 113g) room temp unsalted butter

¾ cup (150g) granulated sugar

¼ cup (50g) light brown sugar

2 room temp large eggs

the how-to: peach layer

1 Preheat the oven to 350°F and grease the sides of a 9-inch round cake pan.

2 In a small bowl, stir together the melted butter and brown sugar until smooth. Spread the mixture evenly onto the bottom of your cake pan. Arrange the peach slices on top of the butter mixture.

the how-to: cake

1 In a medium bowl, whisk together the flour, baking powder, and salt.

2 In a glass measuring cup or small bowl, stir together the bourbon, vanilla extract, and milk.

3 In the bowl of a stand mixer, cream together the butter, granulated sugar, and brown sugar on medium-high speed until light and fluffy, about 3 minutes. Beat in the eggs on medium-high speed, one at a time, until thoroughly combined. Scrape down the bottom and sides of the bowl. With the mixer running on low, add in the flour mixture and milk mixture in two alternating batches, starting and ending

with the flour mixture. Scrape down the bottom and sides of the bowl one more time.

4 Spread the batter evenly into your prepared pan and smooth the top.

5 Bake for 30 to 34 minutes, until the cake is golden brown and a tester inserted in the center comes out clean. Let the cake cool for 10 minutes in the pan, then run a butter knife around the edges to loosen it. Turn it out onto a wire rack, leaving the pan on top of the cake. Wait for 30 seconds, then lift the pan off. Let cool completely before serving. This one's really yummy with ice cream! Store at room temp in an airtight container for up to 3 days.

HOMESICK

～～～

YOU MIGHT BE FEELING:
*out of place, you're longing
for the familiar*

～～～

Homesickness must be one of the most universal feelings there is. We can be homesick for lots of things, not just our physical homes. You can be homesick for a person, homesick for a previous self/life, even homesick for a particular feeling. When you're homesick, you're probably also longing for comfort, familiarity, ease. Or maybe you're longing to be known or understood. Homesickness just ties into so many other feelings. And it's deeply entwined, like memory in general, with the senses!

While your cookies are in the oven, here's a list of suggested activities to help you feel your way through the homesickness:

Watch your comfort show or movie (mine's Meryl Streep's *It's Complicated*).

Wrap yourself in that one blanket that's somehow followed you around your whole life.

Call your sibling to reminisce on a family story that never gets old.

Make a meal that you grew up eating/your family likes to share.

Light a candle that smells like home.

Put on a playlist that reminds you of who you are.

Visit the Cheesecake Factory (this is a joke but also not—I grew up in the suburban Midwest).

sour cream sugar cookies

MAKES ABOUT 14 COOKIES

These cookies taste very much like the sugar cookies you used to buy from those cookie stores at the mall, in the best way. They are a perfect antidote to homesickness, because they taste exactly the same everywhere. They're rolled in crunchy rainbow sanding sugar, get their distinctive flavor from a surprise ingredient—sour cream—and have a lot of vanilla extract (it's all necessary)!

Regardless of where you happen to be right now, when you take a bite of one of these, close your eyes and picture the mall with the Claire's where you got your ears pierced when you were eight. Feel transported to home.

FOR THE COOKIE DOUGH

2½ cups (325g) all-purpose flour
1 teaspoon baking soda
½ teaspoon cream of tartar
½ teaspoon kosher salt
¾ cup (1½ sticks, 170g) room temp unsalted butter
¼ cup (60g) sour cream
1½ cups (300g) granulated sugar
1 large egg
1 tablespoon vanilla extract

FOR THE COATING

½ cup (100g) rainbow sanding/sparkling sugar

SAD

the how-to

1 Preheat the oven to 350°F and line a baking sheet with parchment paper.

2 In a medium bowl, whisk together the flour, baking soda, cream of tartar, and salt.

3 In the bowl of a stand mixer, cream together the butter, sour cream, and granulated sugar on medium-high speed until light and fluffy, about 2 minutes. Beat in the egg and vanilla extract. Add the flour mixture and mix on low speed just until the dough comes together.

4 Form into 3-tablespoon (60g) balls. Roll each ball in sanding sugar, completely covering all of the surfaces.

5 Place the cookies at least 3 inches apart on the baking sheet. Bake for 13 to 15 minutes, until set. Let the cookies cool on the pan for 2 minutes, then transfer them to a wire rack. Store at room temp in an airtight container for up to 2 days.

If you're feeling hopeless right now, please repeat the following phrase to yourself a few times:

Today is just one day.

If I'm feeling hopeless, it's often at the end of a very long or very hard day. So, I want you to make these cookies as the last thing you do before you climb in bed, all eye-masked up. It can be super helpful to end the day by doing something creative. By making something, you're literally creating possibility.

Whatever you're feeling right now is temporary. Sometimes my thoughts get so overwhelming that I feel like I must have always felt like this and will continue to always feel like this. But it's not true! The great thing is, as humans, we have to sleep. It's a tired expression, I know, but tomorrow actually is always another day.

OK, one more suggestion before you go to sleep: text a friend you haven't seen for a while and ask if they want to do something this week.

Psst: If you've already made my funnel cake recipe, take a minute and revisit what you wrote in your notebook from the prompt on the "Excited" page!

peanut butter snickerdoodles

MAKES A BAKER'S DOZEN (13)

This recipe combines two of my very favorite kinds of cookies: peanut butter and snickerdoodle. The origin story is simple: one day I was making a batch of each type of cookie simultaneously and wondered what they might taste like together. As it turns out, they are delicious. These are big but thin cookies. They have crisp edges, with some chew in the middle. A mash-up of the best of both worlds!

If you're making these right before bed, like I think you might, be sure to eat one straight out of the oven paired with a glass of milk (oat milk, or whatever). Don't forget to text your friend!

FOR THE COOKIE DOUGH

1½ cups (195g) all-purpose flour

1 teaspoon baking soda

½ teaspoon kosher salt

½ teaspoon cream of tartar

½ teaspoon ground cinnamon

½ cup (1 stick, 113g) room temp unsalted butter

½ cup (125g) creamy peanut butter (not natural)

1¼ cups (250g) granulated sugar

¼ cup (50g) light brown sugar

1 large egg

2 teaspoons vanilla extract

2 tablespoons water

½ cup (100g) granulated sugar

2 teaspoons ground cinnamon

the how-to: cookie dough

1 Preheat the oven to 350°F and line a baking sheet with foil, dull side up.

2 In a medium bowl, whisk together the flour, baking soda, salt, cream of tartar, and cinnamon.

3 In the bowl of a stand mixer, cream together the butter, peanut butter, granulated sugar, and brown sugar on medium-high speed until creamy, about 2 minutes. Scrape down the sides of the bowl. Beat in the egg, vanilla extract, and water on medium speed until thoroughly combined. Add the flour mixture all at once and mix on low speed until the dough comes together.

4 Form the dough into 3-tablespoon (60g) sized balls.

the how-to: coating

In a small bowl, combine the granulated sugar and cinnamon. Roll each ball in the cinnamon sugar, completely covering all of the surfaces. Place the cookies at least 3 inches apart on the baking sheet. Bake for 15 to 17 minutes, until crisp around the edges and just set in the middle. Let the cookies cool on the pan for 2 minutes, then transfer them to a wire rack. Store at room temp in an airtight container for up to 2 days.

Sometimes I find myself wanting to stay with (or revisit) an unpleasant emotion, even if it doesn't particularly serve me. Either because doing so is a part of a cycle I'm stuck in, or because that emotion is what feels most familiar. For me, one of those emotions is inadequacy. For you, it might be melancholy or anger or regret—the particular blend of emotions we circle back to frequently is unique to us.

Unchecked, the tiny voice in my head loves to provide a running dialogue of self-criticisms and doubts. It can be exhausting. So here are some thoughts to consider adding to your repertoire:

You are doing way more
than you realize.

Even if you did nothing
at all, you would still be worthy of
love and affection.

Life is hard, and you deserve
help anytime you need it.

You cannot possibly fix everything.

Think of how proud/excited
your former selves must be about how
far you've come!

plain old white cake

Yes, we're making white cake with vanilla frosting today. But there is nothing plain about this cake. For starters, the frosting is actually Swiss buttercream, which is my go-to. It's vaguely fancy without trying to be. The cake is scented with almond and vanilla extracts and has a very soft, tender, and fluffy crumb.

This deliciously simple one-layer cake might be the easiest part of your day. It's what I like to make when I'm trying to remind myself that not everything has to be overanalyzed, super complex, or picture-perfect.

FOR THE CAKE

3 large room temp egg whites
1⅔ cups (216g) cake flour
1½ teaspoons baking powder
½ teaspoon kosher salt
½ cup (1 stick, 113g) room temp unsalted butter
1 cup (200g) granulated sugar
1½ teaspoons vanilla extract
¼ teaspoon almond extract
½ cup room temp whole milk

FOR THE BUTTERCREAM

2 large egg whites
½ cup (100g) granulated sugar
¾ cup (1½ sticks, 170g) room temp unsalted butter
2 teaspoons vanilla extract

the how-to: cake

1　Preheat the oven to 350°F and line the bottom of an 8-inch round cake pan with parchment paper. Grease the pan and parchment paper.

2　In the bowl of a stand mixer fitted with the whisk attachment, beat the egg whites on high speed until stiff peaks form. Transfer the egg white mixture to another bowl and wipe out the stand mixer bowl.

3　In a medium bowl, whisk together the cake flour, baking powder, and salt.

4　In the bowl of the stand mixer fitted with the paddle attachment, beat the butter on medium-high speed for about 2 minutes, until smooth. Pour in the granulated sugar and beat on medium-high speed for about 3 minutes, until very light and fluffy. Scrape down the sides of the bowl. Add the vanilla extract and almond extract and mix on medium speed until combined. Add the flour and milk in two alternating batches, starting and ending with the flour. Using a rubber spatula, fold in the egg whites just until no white streaks remain.

5　Pour the batter into your prepared pan and smooth the top.

6　Bake for 32 to 36 minutes, until a tester comes out with moist (but not wet!) crumbs. Cool for 10 minutes in the pan, then turn the cake out onto a wire rack to cool completely.

the how-to: buttercream

1　Heat a large pot of water until simmering. Whisk together the egg whites and granulated sugar in a heatproof metal bowl that fits over the pot. Place the bowl over the simmering water (making sure the water doesn't actually touch the bowl). Keep whisking until you can't feel the sugar if you (carefully, it's hot!) rub it between your fingertips, 2 to 3 minutes.

2　Transfer the egg white mixture to the bowl of a stand mixer. Using the whisk attachment, beat on medium-high speed until the mixture doubles in size, turns glossy, and soft peaks form, about 5 minutes.

3　Add the butter, 2 tablespoons at a time. Continue whipping on medium-high speed until very fluffy, about 5 minutes. Add the vanilla extract and whip until combined.

4　Once the cake is completely cooled, frost with an offset spatula! I like to frost just the top in pretty swooshes and leave the sides of the cake unfrosted. Store in the fridge, covered, for up to 5 days.

YOU MIGHT BE FEELING:
*like you're not getting what
you deserve, that life isn't fair*

For some reason, one of my mom's favorite snappy words of advice to give when I was growing up was "Jealousy is an ugly, ugly thing." Not "an ugly thing"—"an ugly, *ugly* thing." And I'm not sure exactly what the lesson was meant to be, so I'm guessing here, but maaaaybe something about being grateful for what you've got. Which is fine, but we can skip the scare tactics and just say "let's talk about what we're grateful for!" instead. My mom gives some good advice, but I think this little nugget can retire.

Many of us are taught that jealousy is unattractive, and we should be ashamed of it. But I'm here to tell you that it's just not true. Who cares what other people think about your feelings! It's not even possible for your feelings to be ugly! It is OK to feel **all** of your emotions.

And you do not have to be ashamed of being jealous. Here's your permission to feel it fully, with passion. You don't have to judge yourself for your thoughts. And reminder: no one else is going to judge you, because it's your own brain.

cherry cream cheese muffins

MAKES 12 MUFFINS

I know, I know, muffins aren't the most exciting thing to bake. But not everything has to be super exciting. These muffins are moist but light, studded with cream cheese filling, chopped sweet cherries, and lemon zest. We add a dusting of granulated sugar on top to help create a slightly crunchy, sparkly lid.

With this recipe, I want you to specifically focus on the sour, tangy notes (from the lemon zest and cream cheese) when you take a bite. The point is that a little sourness never hurt anyone. In fact, it can sharpen other flavors—in this case, the sweetness of the cherries. The same is true for jealousy! Maybe your jealousy sharpens your dedication, your resilience, or maybe even your compassion (a leap, but I have faith in you). Jealousy doesn't have to be an ugly thing!

FOR THE FILLING

4 oz (113g) softened cream cheese

1 large egg yolk

2 tablespoons granulated sugar

FOR THE MUFFINS

2 cups (260g) + 1 tablespoon all-purpose flour, divided

2 teaspoons baking powder

1 tablespoon fresh lemon zest

½ teaspoon kosher salt

2 cups (320g) pitted and coarsely chopped sweet cherries (frozen is fine)

½ cup (1 stick, 113g) room temp unsalted butter

1 cup (200g) + 1 tablespoon granulated sugar, divided

2 large eggs

2 teaspoons vanilla extract

½ cup (120g) sour cream

the how-to: filling

In a small bowl, stir together the cream cheese, egg yolk, and granulated sugar until smooth. Set aside until needed.

the how-to: muffins

1. Preheat the oven to 375°F and grease a 12-cup muffin tin.

2. In a medium bowl, whisk together 2 cups (260g) of the flour, the baking powder, lemon zest, and salt.

3. In a small bowl, stir together the cherries and the remaining 1 tablespoon of flour. Set aside until needed.

4. In the bowl of a stand mixer fitted with the paddle attachment, cream together the butter and 1 cup (200g) of the granulated sugar on medium-high speed until light and fluffy, about 3 minutes. Scrape down the bowl. Add in the eggs one at a time. Add the vanilla extract and mix until combined. With the mixer running on low speed, add half of the flour mixture, then the sour cream, then the other half of the flour mixture. Gently fold in the cherries with a rubber spatula.

5. Spoon batter into each muffin well, filling the well up halfway. Top with a heaping teaspoonful of the cream cheese filling. Spoon the remaining half of the batter on top of the cream cheese filling. Sprinkle with the remaining 1 tablespoon of granulated sugar.

6. Bake for 25 to 28 minutes, until the tops of the muffins are golden brown. Cool for 5 minutes in the pan, then transfer the muffins to a wire rack to cool completely. Store at room temp in an airtight container for up to 2 days.

For a long time—and sometimes still—I thought that experiences were less valid if they weren't shared. This, of course, isn't true. But life can get pretty lonely sometimes. And even if you're not alone physically, you might still feel alone in your experiences, thoughts, or feelings.

I had an abortion when I was twenty-one. I lived in rural Iowa. I had heard exactly one person share their abortion story before. At the time, I was extremely worried about shame and stigma, and I told almost no one. Years later, I worked up the courage to claim my experience both privately and publicly. It scared me a lot. But when I started sharing my abortion story, it was like a light switched on. As I shared my story, other people started sharing their stories with me. There is a huge benefit to sharing our experiences.

My point is that if you're feeling lonely, it's likely that someone can relate to your experience. It may not be exactly the same—you are your own unique amazing specific person, after all! But there is absolutely enough common shared experience to dispel the myth that we're alone out here.

s'mores rice krispie treats

MAKES 9 LARGE-ISH RICE KRISPIE TREATS

Rice Krispie treats are the definition of a shareable dessert. And, I mean, think about it, have you ever eaten s'mores alone? So, your job is to share these with someone you love (or just like). You're going to make someone's day.

This recipe comes together quickly (fifteen minutes tops), feels fancy without trying, and you probably already have Rice Krispies in your pantry (just me?). It's a continuation of my predilection for adding graham crackers to anything I can. The trick here is to not pack the mixture down into the pan—just gently nudge it in, and you'll wind up with light and fluffy treats.

6 tablespoons (85g) unsalted butter
5½ cups (one 10-oz package, 283g) mini marshmallows
¼ teaspoon vanilla extract
a pinch of kosher salt
3 cups (90g) Rice Krispies cereal
1 cup (120g) graham cracker pieces
½ cup (70g) chopped milk chocolate

the how-to

1 Line the bottom and two sides of an 8-inch square baking pan with an overhanging strip of parchment paper cut to the width of the bottom of the pan. Grease the exposed sides of the pan and parchment paper.

2 In a large pot, melt the butter over medium heat. Heat, stirring, until the butter turns a deep amber

color and smells nutty (watch it carefully—
don't let it burn!). As soon as your butter
is browned, add the marshmallows and
stir until smooth. Turn off the heat. Stir in
the vanilla extract and salt. Add the Rice
Krispies and graham cracker pieces and stir
until completely coated.

3 Transfer the mixture to your prepared pan.
Gently spread it out into an even layer, but
don't press it down (we don't want dense
Rice Krispie treats!).

4 Scatter the chopped chocolate over the
top. Let cool for an hour, then cut into 9
squares and eat.

note: I typically use an actual chocolate bar for this recipe!

YOU MIGHT BE FEELING:
*like it's just not going
to work out; like there's
no point in trying*

Yes, sometimes things don't work out. But I know that you will be able to deal with it. You are strong and capable, and you can figure things out. (PS: This beautiful piece of wisdom comes pretty much word for word from my therapist.)

It is really, really difficult when things work out differently than you'd planned or hoped or dreamed. (As someone who once received an acceptance email from a college and then one hour later received a "We're very sorry, that was actually meant to be a rejection" email from a college—I know what I'm talking about.) If you've endured a streak of hard, painful things, it makes complete sense that you are feeling pessimistic. You're protecting yourself. You're responding to a pattern. But I'm here to remind you that you deserve wonderful and beautiful things. And that those beautiful and wonderful things exist.

Can you take a minute to grab your notebook to make a brief list of things you love/like/or at a minimum don't loathe entirely? And if you're stumped: at the very least, you probably don't loathe the movie 10 *Things I Hate About You* (seriously, who could loathe a Heath Ledger/Julia Stiles pairing?).

butterscotch cake with salted honey buttercream

MAKES AN 8-INCH SQUARE SINGLE-LAYER CAKE

You know what's an antidote to pessimism? Cake! Cake reminds us of celebrating, or growing a year older, or finishing a romantic meal. It's difficult to maintain a gloomy outlook with frosting in your mouth. Also, it's impossible to scowl while saying butterscotch. Really—we're going to test it.

This recipe makes a single-layer cake flavored with dark brown sugar and vanilla and moistened by sour cream. But the real star of the show is the salted honey Swiss buttercream. Fluffy from the egg whites, smooth from the butter, and rich from the honey—it's shockingly yummy. Plus that little pinch of flaky salt! Chef's kiss.

FOR THE CAKE

1½ cups (195g) all-purpose flour
1½ teaspoons baking powder
½ teaspoon kosher salt
6 tablespoons (85g) room temp unsalted butter
1 cup (200g) dark brown sugar
¼ cup (60g) sour cream
½ cup heavy cream
1 large egg
1½ teaspoons vanilla extract

2 large egg whites

½ cup (100 grams) granulated sugar

¾ cup (1½ sticks, 170g) room temp unsalted butter

2 tablespoons honey

½ teaspoon flaky salt (such as Maldon) + more for sprinkling

the how-to: cake

1　Preheat the oven to 350°F. Line the bottom and two sides of an 8-inch square cake pan with an overhanging strip of parchment paper cut to the width of the bottom of the pan. Grease the exposed sides of the pan and parchment paper.

2　In a medium bowl, whisk together the flour, baking powder, and kosher salt.

3　In the bowl of a stand mixer, cream together the butter and brown sugar on medium speed for 2 minutes, until light and fluffy. Add the sour cream, heavy cream, egg, and vanilla extract. Beat on medium speed until mixed. Pour in the dry ingredient mixture and mix on low speed just until incorporated.

4　Bake for 30 to 35 minutes, until a tester inserted in the middle comes out clean. Cool for 10 minutes in the pan, then turn the cake out onto a wire rack to cool completely.

the how-to: swiss buttercream

1　Heat a large pot of water until simmering. Whisk together the egg whites and granulated sugar in a heatproof metal bowl that fits over the pot. Wearing an oven mitt, place the bowl over the simmering water (making sure the water doesn't actually touch the bowl). Keep whisking until you can't feel the sugar if you rub it (carefully! It's hot!) between your fingertips, 2 to 3 minutes.

2　Transfer the egg white mixture to the bowl of a stand mixer. Using the whisk attachment, beat on medium-high speed until the mixture doubles in size, turns glossy, and soft peaks form, about 5 minutes.

3　Add the butter, 2 tablespoons at a time. Continue beating on medium-high speed until very fluffy, about 5 minutes. Add the honey and flaky salt and whip until combined.

4　Once the cake is completely cooled, plop the frosting on the top and spread it out to the edges using an offset spatula, making decorative swirls. Lightly sprinkle with more flaky salt, if desired. Store in the fridge, covered, for up to 5 days.

YOU MIGHT BE FEELING:
*not good enough; regret
for having tried*

Rejection flat-out sucks, and it's extremely hard not to take it personally. You put yourself out there and it didn't work out, and that can be really painful. There's a popular narrative that rejection is "just part of life." And while that's true, it certainly doesn't help us in the moment of rejection! *Everything* is part of life, but it doesn't mean you have to discount the way you feel.

So, I want to honor that feeling. Let's try something real quick. Find a pen and a piece of scrap paper, any scrap paper (maybe that grocery store receipt crumpled in your bag?). Now write down the person/entity/whatever that rejected you. Write down (the gist of!) what they said/did/didn't do. Now re-crumple the paper dramatically and throw it in the trash even more dramatically. I know it might seem goofy, but sometimes this helps me grab ahold of and release a rejection that's swirling around repeatedly in my mind. Now: let's turn on the oven!

lime zest meltaways

MAKES ABOUT 32 COOKIES

Lime (either eating it or smelling it) always seems to bring me out of a funk. It has properties that counteract feelings of rejection, I'm pretty sure (this is not science). When lime zest hits my nose, my mood lifts, however momentarily. So grab that zester and get ready.

We're continuing with the theme of letting things go with this recipe—these babies literally melt in your mouth. They're a light and buttery cookie with a wash of sweet, limey glaze over the top. I use coconut oil to keep them moist, but don't worry—the flavor isn't overpowering!

FOR THE COOKIES

2 cups (260g) all-purpose flour
½ teaspoon baking powder
½ teaspoon kosher salt
2 teaspoons fresh lime zest
¾ cup (150g) granulated sugar
½ cup (1 stick, 113g) room temp unsalted butter
½ cup (100g) room temp (not melted!) virgin coconut oil
1 large egg
½ teaspoon vanilla extract

FOR THE GLAZE

1½ cups (180g) powdered sugar
2 tablespoons fresh lime juice
1 tablespoon whole milk

SAD

the how-to: cookies

1 Preheat the oven to 375°F and line a baking sheet with parchment paper.

2 In a medium bowl, whisk together the flour, baking powder, and salt.

3 In the bowl of a stand mixer, rub the lime zest into the granulated sugar (this will help release more flavor from the zest!). Add the butter and coconut oil and cream on medium-high speed until very creamy, about 3 minutes. Beat in the egg and vanilla extract on medium speed until combined. Add the flour mixture and mix on low speed until just combined.

4 Roll the dough into 1-tablespoon (20g) balls. Place them 2 inches apart on your prepared baking sheet.

5 Bake for 8 to 9 minutes, until the center is set (don't overbake these—they will still look pale when they're done!). Let the cookies sit on the sheet for 2 minutes, then transfer them to a cooling rack. Let cool before glazing.

the how-to: glaze

While cookies are baking, make your glaze. In a medium bowl, whisk together the powdered sugar, lime juice, and milk. When the cookies have cooled completely, dip the tops in the glaze. Store at room temp in an airtight container for up to 3 days.

When I'm feeling down, my mind defaults to labeling the feeling as sadness even if it's actually a different feeling, like loneliness, pessimism, or inadequacy. Sometimes it's easier to shorthand my feelings as "sadness" instead of trying to untangle the full complexity of what I'm feeling. But sometimes we are, in fact, just straight-up sad. I'm so proud of you for recognizing your feelings and navigating your way through the hard stuff.

You might've been taught to push your sadness down and put on a brave face for the (supposed!) benefit of people around you. Or maybe you were even told it was for your *own* benefit—that if you gave your sadness any space, it would swallow you whole. But here's a reminder if you need it: exploring your sadness is not wallowing in it, and the real bravery comes from going through it, not around.

chocolate olive oil cake

MAKES A STANDARD LOAF CAKE

This loaf cake has a little bit of everything thrown in: Dutch-process cocoa powder, dark brown sugar, olive oil, buttermilk, semisweet chocolate, espresso powder, and even boiling water. Similarly, when we're sad, it's more than OK to bring out all the comfort options. Might I suggest: fluffy socks, a cup of peppermint tea, your childhood quilt/stuffed animal/comfort object, a weighted blanket, putting up your Christmas tree no matter what time of year it is, snuggling your pet, running a hot bath. Try combining a few of them! Be gentle with yourself today—you deserve all the ease and comfort in the world. (On that front, no need to fire up the stand mixer here—a whisk will do just fine).

FOR THE CAKE

1⅔ cups (216g) all-purpose flour

⅓ cup (30g) Dutch-process cocoa powder

1½ teaspoons baking powder

1½ teaspoons espresso powder

½ teaspoon kosher salt

1 cup (200g) dark brown sugar

2 large eggs

1 cup olive oil

⅓ cup buttermilk

2 teaspoons vanilla extract

½ cup boiling water

⅔ cup (93g) chopped semisweet chocolate

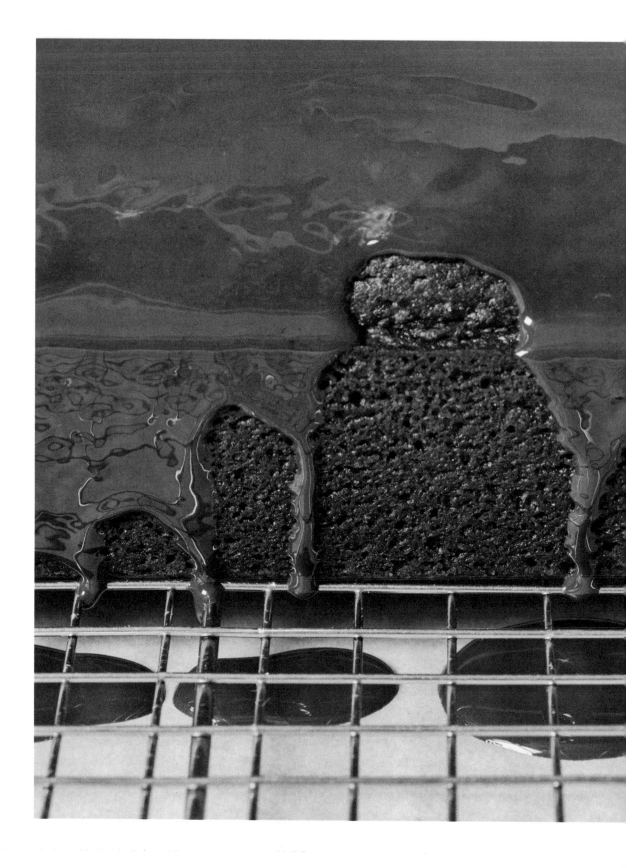

½ cup (70g) chopped semisweet chocolate

1 tablespoon Dutch-process cocoa powder

2 tablespoons olive oil

a pinch of flaky salt (such as Maldon)

the how-to: cake

1 Preheat the oven to 350°F. Line the bottom and two sides of a 9 x 5-inch loaf pan with a strip of parchment paper. Grease the parchment paper and exposed sides.

2 In a medium bowl, whisk together the flour, cocoa powder, baking powder, espresso powder, and kosher salt.

3 In a large heatproof bowl, whisk together the brown sugar and eggs until smooth. Add the olive oil, buttermilk, and vanilla extract and whisk until fully combined. Stir in the flour mixture using a rubber spatula, until just combined. Carefully stir in the boiling water. Fold in the chopped chocolate. Pour the batter into your prepared loaf pan and smooth the top with an offset spatula.

4 Bake for 55 to 60 minutes, until a toothpick inserted in the center comes out clean. Let the cake cool in the pan for 10 minutes, then turn it out onto a wire rack to cool completely.

the how-to: glaze

1 In a medium heatproof bowl, combine the semisweet chocolate, cocoa powder, olive oil, and flaky salt. Microwave in 30-second increments, stirring in between, until smooth. Pour the glaze evenly over the cooled cake.

2 Store at room temp in an airtight container for up to 3 days, or in the fridge for up to a week.

Sorrow is such an intense and painful feeling, it might even seem like you can feel it in your bones. During my worst breakup, I found it almost impossible to do anything for more than two minutes without the sorrow breaking through. Each time, it felt like I'd had the wind knocked out of me. The only place I could manage to go was the yoga studio, and I learned a breathing exercise there that I want to share with you now. It's really simple. Breathe in slowly through your nose for four counts, then breathe out for eight counts. Set a timer on your phone (or your kitchen timer!) for two minutes, and continue breathing like this, and then come back here. How do you feel? Is your body calmer? Is your mind a little lighter? I hope so.

You made it through two minutes. Now let's try for two more.

raspberry tahini linzers

MAKES 15 TO 20 COOKIES, DEPENDING ON CUTTER SIZE

Free yourself of the holiday cookie vs. non–holiday cookie dichotomy! You can have any cookie any time of the year. I promise. Today we're making something kind of fussy, but the end result is just so *cute.* The cookies themselves have a deep flavor (hello tahini!), which is brightened by a sprinkle of powdered sugar and a dollop of raspberry jam sandwiched in the middle. Typically ground nuts are used in linzers, but I love the more complex but still-nutty vibe you get by using tahini instead. I like making these as a meditative, uplifting, and delicious activity when I'm going through it. And: using cookie cutters to cut out fun shapes can help invoke a much-needed childlike levity.

FOR THE COOKIES

1¾ cups (228g) all-purpose flour

¼ teaspoon kosher salt

1 teaspoon ground cinnamon

½ cup (1 stick, 113g) room temp unsalted butter

½ cup (113g) tahini

¾ cup (150g) granulated sugar

1 teaspoon fresh lemon zest

½ cup (60g) powdered sugar, divided

1 large egg

½ teaspoon vanilla extract

FOR THE FILLING

½ cup (150g) seedless raspberry jam

the how-to: cookies

1 In a medium bowl, whisk together the flour, salt, and cinnamon.

2 In the bowl of a stand mixer fitted with the paddle attachment, beat the butter, tahini, granulated sugar, lemon zest, and ¼ cup (30g) of the powdered sugar on medium speed until creamy, about 3 minutes. Beat in the egg and vanilla extract. Stir in the dry ingredients on low speed.

3 Divide the dough in half. Roll out each half between two sheets of wax paper or parchment paper to ¼ inch thick. Refrigerate the rolled-out dough for at least 1½ hours (or freeze for 45 minutes!). Meanwhile, preheat the oven to 350°F and line a baking sheet with parchment paper.

4 Using a 2-inch cutter (personally, I like stars and heart shapes!), cut shapes out of the dough. Place on the baking sheet and bake for 8 to 10 minutes, until the edges are beginning to brown. Transfer to a wire rack and let cool completely. Repeat with the remaining cookies.

the how-to: filling & assembly

Divide the cooled cookies in half. Using a fine-mesh sieve, sprinkle the tops of one half with the remaining ¼ cup (30g) of powdered sugar. Spread a heaping ½ teaspoonful of jam on the bottoms of the other half. Sandwich them together, powdered sugared cookies on top. Store at room temp in an airtight container for up to 5 days.

mad

The recipes in this chapter are here to support you with big and often uncomfortable feelings.

Vibes: The sound of a car door slamming, the color red, your face turning hot

Let's get one thing straight: being mad doesn't make you an ungrateful or negative person. I grew up believing that anger was an uncontrollable force that welled up inside of you and eventually exploded, likely harming the people around you in the process. But now I know that I can be mad *and* effectively communicate what I need. I know that I can feel it, listen to it, and then release it. Of course, this is much easier said than done, because big feelings often seem to take over our minds and bodies, overriding our thoughts and actions.

When I'm mad, sometimes it helps me to take a tiny step back and approach the feeling from a place of curiosity and explore why I might be feeling this way. Have I been reminded of a past negative experience? Is something threatening me, my sense of self, or someone I care about? Am I not being treated in the way I deserve? These are all triggers for me to get mad, and maybe they are for you too.

Now, consider how you might respond to your best friend if they were feeling mad. What would you tell them? You'd probably say something along the lines of: "I'm sorry things are hard right now, and I'm here for you." Or you might say something like, "Yeah, that completely, totally sucks and you shouldn't have to deal with it." Would you judge them for feeling the way they do? Most likely not! You deserve this same level of care and understanding.

mad

angry

annoyed

furious

bitter

grouchy

moody

insulted

selfish

stubborn

vengeful

YOU MIGHT BE FEELING:
*like you want to smash
something or run away to live in
an oceanside cottage by yourself*

Anger is one of the most famous emotions in part because it's so very normal. I know a lot of the time we try to swallow the anger back down, but for today, how about you give yourself some space to fully feel it? Remember, no matter how bad your feelings might feel, they are not "bad," and feeling them does not make *you* "bad." Sitting with your anger without avoiding it or numbing it can help expand your capacity for self-compassion and strengthen your ability to effectively process it.

In the meantime, though, I give you my full blessing and encouragement to slam cabinet doors, whisk at a *very* brisk pace, get flour all over everything, and express your flavor of anger in the physical world.

chocolate graham cracker cookies

MAKES ABOUT 20 COOKIES

This recipe started out as an accident, really. I had a lot of graham cracker crumbs left over from testing another recipe (I think it was the butterscotch pie?) and was tinkering around with a new chocolate cookie. At the last second, I threw in the leftover crumbs. And it worked! The graham cracker just adds a little something extra, both texture-wise and flavor-wise.

This recipe is perfect for when you're angry because we're going to get some of that furious energy out by smashing things with a rolling pin! I've recently discovered that you can buy graham cracker crumbs pre-smashed. But I really prefer to smash them myself, and I recommend that you do so as well. Just put the whole graham crackers in a large Ziploc bag, seal it (making sure to get any trapped air out!), put it on the counter, and smash it with something heavy. As I mentioned, I use a wooden rolling pin, but any number of objects will work. Smash away! Make noise!

2¼ cups (293g) all-purpose flour

½ cup (45g) Dutch-process cocoa powder

1 teaspoon baking soda

¾ teaspoon kosher salt

1 cup (2 sticks, 227g) room temp unsalted butter

½ cup (100g) granulated sugar

½ cup (100g) light brown sugar

1 large egg

1 large egg yolk

2 teaspoons vanilla extract

1½ cups (150g) graham cracker crumbs, a mix of small-ish pieces and finer crumbs, divided

the how-to

1 Preheat the oven to 350°F and line a baking sheet with parchment paper.

2 In a medium bowl, whisk together the flour, cocoa powder, baking soda, and salt.

3 In the bowl of a stand mixer fitted with the paddle attachment, cream together the butter, granulated sugar, and brown sugar on medium-high speed until creamy, about 2 minutes. Beat in the egg, egg yolk, and vanilla extract. Turn off the mixer and add the flour mixture. Mix on low speed just until the dough comes together. Add ½ cup of the graham cracker pieces and mix just until combined.

4 Form the dough into 2-tablespoon (40g) balls. Roll each ball in the remaining 1 cup of graham cracker pieces, completely covering all of the surfaces.

5 Place the cookies at least 3 inches apart on the baking sheet. Flatten each one slightly using the bottom of a glass or your palm. Bake for 10 to 12 minutes, until set around the edges but still soft in the middle. Let the cookies cool on the pan for 2 minutes, then transfer them to a wire rack. Store at room temp in an airtight container for up to 3 days.

ANNOYED

~~~

YOU MIGHT BE FEELING:
*like your eyes are rolling
of their own volition*

~~~

I'm someone who is quick to annoyance. Little things can throw off my entire day—when my socks feel wrong, or I forget my sunglasses, or another driver honks at me—these things do not roll off my back easily. While sometimes feelings of annoyance come from these general life inconveniences, they are also commonly the product of miscommunication or misunderstanding. So sometimes it helps me to remember that (most) people are not doing things with the purpose of annoying me. If I have the bandwidth, I do my best to step out of an adversarial mindset and into a slightly more compassionate one, i.e., "They probably had a shitty day at work, and I like to honk at people too." (Side note: I'm a city driver, and I deeply understand the desire to honk back at the person who honked at you.)

To be clear: I'm not suggesting that you should just swallow your frustration. Just try not to hold on to it so tightly that it ruins the *entire* day when you could be focusing on the yummy (if I do say so myself) donuts you're about to make.

blueberry buttermilk donuts

~~~

MAKES 20 DONUTS + 20 DONUT HOLES

If there's one thing you should know about me, it's that I love donuts. Like, *love* donuts. When I was a child, strawberry iced cake donuts were my jam. In fact, some of my fondest childhood memories involve sitting on a stool at the counter of our local donut shop, swinging my feet. It seemed straight out of the '50s in there—entirely decorated in soft shades of pink, yellow, and orange. The warm, sweet smell was incredible. When the swinging door would open, you could see the donuts being made in the back. Unsurprisingly, this fascinated me. I can still taste the sweet pink icing I licked off my fingertips.

Much later, I learned to make donuts myself. Frying donuts at home takes some careful attention, but it is 100 percent doable. The most important thing about making donuts (as stress-free as possible) is that you have everything prepped and ready to go before you start. You're frying things in hot oil—we want to make sure everything's within reach. Donut worry, I'll walk you through it.

FOR THE DONUTS

4 cups (520g) all-purpose flour

¾ cup (150g) granulated sugar

1 tablespoon baking powder

¾ teaspoon kosher salt

¼ teaspoon ground nutmeg

1 cup (150g) coarsely chopped blueberries,
fresh or frozen

¾ cup (180g) sour cream

¾ cup buttermilk

4 tablespoons (½ stick, 57g) melted and
cooled unsalted butter

1 large egg

2 large egg yolks

2 teaspoons vanilla extract

about 6 cups vegetable shortening or
vegetable oil (I prefer shortening), for frying

FOR THE GLAZE

2 cups (240g) powdered sugar

¼ cup buttermilk

1 teaspoon vanilla extract

the how-to: donuts

1   Line two baking sheets with parchment
paper, line two wire cooling racks with
paper towels, and thoroughly flour your
countertop.

2   In an extra-large bowl, whisk together the
flour, granulated sugar, baking powder, salt,
and nutmeg. Add the blueberries and stir
to combine.

3   In a medium bowl, whisk together the sour
cream, buttermilk, melted butter, egg, egg
yolks, and vanilla extract until smooth.

4   Make a well in the center of the dry
ingredients and pour the wet ingredients
in. Stir with a rubber spatula to roughly
combine, then switch to gently kneading
with your hands until the dough comes
together into a cohesive mass—this should
take only a few kneads. Turn the dough
out onto your floured countertop. Using
your palms, pat the dough out to a ½-inch
thickness. If the dough is sticking, add
a bit more flour underneath. Sprinkle

some more flour lightly over the top of
the dough. Cut out donut shapes about 3
inches wide—you can use a donut cutter,
cookie cutter, or the rim of a glass. Use a
second 1-inch-wide cutter (or a shot glass!)
to make donut holes in the center of each
donut. Transfer the donuts and donut holes
to the prepared baking sheets. Reroll the
scraps as needed until all the dough has
been cut. If you run out of room for full-
sized donuts at the very end, switch to just
donut holes. Put the donut-laden baking
sheets in the fridge to chill for 20 minutes.

the how-to: glaze

In a medium bowl, whisk together the
powdered sugar, buttermilk, and vanilla
extract. You're looking for a thick-ish paste-
like consistency, where the glaze can still
move around the bowl freely. To thin, add
another teaspoon of buttermilk. Set aside for
later.

the how-to: frying & assembly

1   About 10 minutes into the chilling time,
start heating your shortening or oil. In a
Dutch oven or cast-iron skillet (you'll need
a depth of about 1½ inches) with a candy
thermometer clipped to the side, heat the
shortening over medium heat. When it
reaches 365°F, you're ready to start frying.
Make sure your paper towel–lined baking
sheets are within easy reach of your stove
and your tongs are in your hand.

2   Fry the donuts a few at a time (in my
Dutch oven, I do four at a time) for 1½ to
2 minutes per side (use heatproof tongs
to flip them over halfway through), until
deeply golden.

3   Drain the donuts on your prepped paper towel–lined wire rack. Let them rest until they are cool enough to handle (like 2-ish minutes), then dip the tops of the warm donuts into the glaze.

4   Repeat with the rest of the donuts, then fry the donut holes. For the holes, you'll only need to fry them for about a minute a side. Dip the donut holes into the glaze. Admire your work. Best eaten day of!

note: If the shortening gets too hot in the midst of frying, just turn the stove off for a few minutes until it comes back down to 365ºF, then turn it back on and resume frying. If it dips down below 365ºF, wait for it to come back up before frying the next batch. Trust me: it'd be a travesty to mess up your perfectly good donuts with oil that's just too hot or too cold.

Bitterness is a complex feeling, and it can actually be considered a secondary emotion—a feeling we have *about* another emotion. If you work backward, you might find that the bitterness you're feeling stems from anger, or fear, or even sadness. So let's take a minute to explore the surrounding feelings a bit more. Use your notebook to write down what you're feeling, and be sure to acknowledge its nuances. Try not to judge what comes up—this is a great opportunity to work on that self-compassion thing (and you're right, it's not easy).

Often, the word *bitter* is used in a dismissive or even derogatory way, with the implication that feeling bitter makes you a poor sport. But it doesn't, and you're not! It's just a feeling, and feelings are human. Sometimes (in baking, and in life), bitterness can help make the sweeter moments pop.

chocolate espresso shortbread

MAKES ABOUT 24 2½-INCH COOKIES

Just like there's no shame in feeling bitter, there's no shame in adding a little bitterness to your baked goods. In fact, much like in life, bitter notes can help to accentuate the sweet ones! This recipe folds a bitter ingredient—espresso powder—into a velvety chocolate shortbread base. The result is a depth of flavor that you couldn't get from the chocolate alone, as the espresso powder helps you elevate the other ingredients. Tiny but mighty! These cookies are slice and bake, which means low effort but high reward. We'll throw in some chopped milk chocolate for a note of pure sweetness.

1½ cups (195g) all-purpose flour

½ cup (45g) Dutch-process cocoa powder

1½ teaspoons espresso powder

1 teaspoon kosher salt

1 cup (2 sticks, 227g) room temp unsalted butter

¾ cup (150g) light brown sugar

1½ teaspoons vanilla extract

5 oz (140g, about 1 cup) finely (but not *super* finely) chopped milk chocolate

the how-to

1 In a medium bowl, whisk together the flour, cocoa powder, espresso powder, and salt. In the bowl of a stand mixer fitted with the paddle attachment,

MAD

cream together the butter, brown sugar, and vanilla extract until light and fluffy, about 3 minutes. Add the dry ingredients and mix on low speed until the dough comes together. Pour in the chocolate chunks and mix until just combined. Scrape the bottom of the bowl with a spatula to make sure everything's mixed in.

2 Divide the dough into two and roll each half into a 1½-inch-wide log. Wrap each log in plastic wrap. The dough will be sticky— you can use the plastic wrap to help even out the log! Refrigerate for 2 hours, or if you're in a hurry, freeze for 30 minutes.

3 Preheat the oven to 350°F and line a baking sheet with parchment paper.

4 Using a sharp knife, cut each dough log into ½-inch rounds. Place the cookies 1 inch apart on the baking sheet. Bake for 11 to 13 minutes, until the edges are set. Let the cookies cool on the pan for 2 minutes, then transfer them to a wire rack. Store at room temp in an airtight container for up to a week.

FURIOUS

≈≈≈≈≈

YOU MIGHT BE FEELING:
a desire to scream at someone
(or just into a pillow)

≈≈≈≈≈

I think this is one of the most intense feelings in this book. Beyond annoyance, frustration, and anger, fury likes to show up for me as a white-hot sensation of rage coursing through my body. It's as if you turned the dial of mad all the way up. When I'm feeling furious, I find it pretty difficult to think about anything else. My thoughts tend to repeat themselves on a loop, reinforcing my fury. It can feel all-consuming.

Now's a great time to try putting just a bit of distance between you and the source of your fury. You don't have to hold on to it so tightly. If you're feeling like you might explode, let's take a dance break. Yes, it sounds silly, but it's a thing. Get your body moving, even if it's just for three minutes. Do whatever feels right—we're not going for the best dance moves here, we're just trying to elevate our heart rate, metabolize some of that adrenaline, and release some of that furious energy. OK cool, now let's bake. (Feel free to bring the music/dancing into the kitchen.)

orange-poppy seed mini scones

MAKES 16 MINI SCONES

Like biscotti, scones have kind of a bad reputation. And it's true, I have eaten many dry and unsatisfying scones in my lifetime. But put those out of your mind, because these little dudes are full of flavor and moisture. They have a hint of almond extract—enough to make you say *hmm, what is that flavor note*, but not enough to make you say *wow, that's really a lot of almond in there.* Then there's orange zest for brightness. And you know what's better than a scone? A mini scone.

If your fury doesn't abate as you bake these scones, I have a suggestion: make yourself breakfast for dinner. Fry up some bacon, scramble some eggs, pour yourself a glass of something, and devour a couple of your freshly baked mini scones. There's just something about breakfast for dinner that can reset my mood. I think maybe it's that my brain doesn't expect it, so it can disrupt those pesky cyclical thought patterns. Give it a go!

FOR THE SCONES

2 teaspoons fresh orange zest
½ cup (100g) granulated sugar
3 cups (390g) all-purpose flour
2 teaspoons baking powder
½ teaspoon kosher salt
1 tablespoon poppy seeds
½ cup (1 stick, 113g) cold unsalted butter, cut into ½-inch cubes

1 cup heavy cream

¼ cup fresh orange juice

1 large egg, beaten

½ teaspoon vanilla extract

¼ teaspoon almond extract

1 cup (120g) powdered sugar

2 to 3 tablespoons fresh orange juice

¼ teaspoon vanilla extract

the how-to: scones

1 Preheat the oven to 375°F and line a large baking sheet with parchment paper.

2 In a large bowl, rub the orange zest into the granulated sugar using your fingertips (this will help release more flavor from the zest!). Add the flour, baking powder, salt, and poppy seeds and whisk until combined. Add the butter chunks and work them into the flour mixture with your fingertips until sandy—the largest pieces should be the size of black beans. Make a well in the center of the dry ingredients and pour in the heavy cream, orange juice, beaten egg, vanilla extract, and almond extract. Use a rubber spatula to stir until it comes together into a shaggy dough.

3 Turn the dough out onto a floured surface and divide it into two equal parts. Pat each part out into a 1-inch-tall circle. Cut each circle into 8 even wedges—you'll end up with 16 scones total! Arrange the scones on your prepared baking sheet—make sure to give them enough room to expand in the oven.

4 Bake for 16 to 18 minutes, until lightly golden. Transfer them to a cooling rack while you make your glaze.

the how-to: glaze

In a small bowl, stir together the powdered sugar, orange juice, and vanilla extract. Set a length of wax paper or parchment paper under your cooling rack to catch any drips. Spoon the glaze over the still-warm scones, letting it drip down the sides. Store at room temp in an airtight container for up to 3 days.

If you're feeling over literally all of it, it's OK to retreat to a place where you don't have to put on airs for the people around you. Give yourself some space to breathe, where you don't need to worry about what people will make of the scowl on your face. Go ahead and glare away.

When I'm feeling grouchy, I like to go to movies by myself. Something about sitting in a dark, air-conditioned theater eating Milk Duds and not speaking to anyone for a couple of hours soothes my soul. But since you're baking today, let's do the next best thing: get your laptop and find a way to stream *When Harry Met Sally* while you make hand pies. This might not be *your* favorite movie, but it *is* mine and I truly believe it can lighten even the grumpiest of moods. Spend some time marveling at Meg Ryan/Sally's autumn-themed outfits and commiserating with Billy Crystal/Harry's grumpy attitude. (Note: Yes, you can replace this with another movie that embraces and celebrates grouchiness—if you must. Just make sure you choose something familiar that helps you wind down.)

banana hand pies

MAKES 12 TO 18 HAND PIES, DEPENDING ON SIZE

I'm one of those people who makes pie when I'm channeling Oscar the Grouch. Maybe you're one of those people too. And if not, you're about to become one! Making pie crust is a great way to channel emotional energy because it's just so hands-on. There's the mashing the butter into the flour, using your muscles to roll out the dough, and pinching those crust edges into place. But these lil' hand pies are special because they don't require digging out your pie plate or dealing with precision. You can make them any shape you want, and they're made to be eaten right out of the oven, still warm. They're big-emotion friendly. Also, there's just something about the bright flavor of banana that uplifts me when I'm in a bad mood.

FOR THE FILLING

⅔ cup mashed ripe banana (from about 2 bananas)

¼ cup (50g) light brown sugar

½ teaspoon vanilla extract

½ teaspoon ground cinnamon

a pinch of kosher salt

2 tablespoons semisweet or milk chocolate chips

FOR THE CRUST

1 recipe Double Pie crust (page 238)

FOR THE EGG WASH

1 large egg

1 tablespoon heavy cream

1 tablespoon sanding sugar, for sprinkling

the how-to: filling

1   Preheat the oven to 375°F and line a baking sheet with parchment paper.

2   In a medium bowl, whisk together the mashed banana, brown sugar, vanilla extract, cinnamon, and salt. Stir in the chocolate chips.

the how-to: crust

Roll out the first disk of pie crust into a rough circle (it should end up being a bit less than ⅛ inch thick). Using a cookie cutter (ideally one that's at least 3 inches wide), cut the dough into circles (or any shape you'd prefer!). Re-roll the scraps and cut out more circles. Place the cut circles on the baking sheet and set it in the fridge to firm up a bit, then roll out the second disk of dough and repeat. Make sure you end up with an even number!

the how-to: assembly

1   In a small bowl, whisk together the egg and heavy cream.

2   Remove the baking sheet from the fridge and add a tablespoonful of filling to the center of half of your cut circles. Rub the edges of these circles with water and place the remaining shapes on top. Press with your fingertips to seal, then use the tines of a fork to frame the edges. Cut a couple of ventilation slits into the top of each mini pie, brush with egg wash, and sprinkle with sanding sugar. Repeat with the remaining pies. Put any pies that are not immediately going into the oven in the fridge.

3   Place the pies on your prepared baking sheet and bake for 20 to 22 minutes, until golden brown. Cool on a wire cooling rack, or eat them right out of the oven! Store at room temp in an airtight container for up to 3 days.

YOU MIGHT BE FEELING:
*offended, misunderstood, like
someone is out to get you*

~~~~~~

Along with rejection, this is one of my personal least favorite emotions to experience. And I suppose they're actually sort of two sides of the same coin. Insult can feel really vulnerable and spikey. You might be feeling misunderstood or mischaracterized. There might also be some embarrassment there. It's really uncomfortable!

It's really, really hard to feel this in the moment, but try to remember that you are *you*, not someone else's perception of you. You can't control what other people think, and their opinions do not determine your worth or value as a person. Like a decadent cake, you are a complex, multilayered being, with so many wonderful qualities. And yes, some more challenging ones too—how very human of you. You are beautiful and your uniqueness and impact on the world can't be replaced.

triple chocolate cake

~~~~~~

MAKES AN 8-INCH THREE-LAYER CAKE

This cake is both triple-layered and triple chocolate. Yes, you need three kinds of chocolate for this recipe. But it is sooo worth it. The cake is *very* chocolatey, and the custard-based frosting tastes exactly like the childhood favorite dirt and worms (that chocolate pudding + Oreos dessert that you might've had in third grade), minus the worms. But if you want to go ahead and add some gummy worms for decoration, I support it.

This is a relatively complex (but not difficult!) recipe. It's meant to complement your beautiful complexity as a person. A good stout beer gives the cake an intense full-bodied flavor—a great match for the intense full-bodied feeling of insult.

FOR THE CAKE

¾ cup stout beer

2 oz (57g) coarsely chopped bittersweet chocolate

1⅔ cups (217g) all-purpose flour

2 cups (400g) granulated sugar

¾ cup (68g) Dutch-process cocoa powder

2 teaspoons baking powder

½ teaspoon baking soda

1 teaspoon kosher salt

4 large eggs

¾ cup vegetable oil

1 tablespoon vanilla extract

½ cup boiling water

½ cup heavy cream

1½ cups (263g) semisweet chocolate chips

¾ cup (150g) granulated sugar

⅓ cup (45g) cornstarch

¼ cup (23g) Dutch-process cocoa powder

scant ¼ teaspoon kosher salt

2 large eggs

1 cup whole milk

1½ cups (3 sticks, 340g) cool room temp
   unsalted butter

2 teaspoons vanilla extract

the how-to: cakes

1 Preheat the oven to 350°F. Line the bottoms of three 8-inch round cake pans with parchment paper. Grease the pans and parchment paper.

2 In a small saucepan, heat the stout over medium-low heat until just simmering. Add the chopped chocolate and stir until smooth. Set aside to cool slightly.

3 In a medium bowl, whisk together the flour, sugar, cocoa powder, baking powder, baking soda, and salt.

4 In a large heatproof bowl, whisk together the eggs, vegetable oil, stout/chocolate mixture, and vanilla extract. Add the dry ingredient mixture and stir with a rubber spatula until thoroughly combined. Pour in the boiling water and carefully stir until smooth.

5 Pour the batter into your prepared cake pans. Bake for 25 to 27 minutes, until a tester inserted in the center comes out with moist crumbs. Let the cakes cool in the pans for 10 minutes, then turn out onto a wire rack to cool completely.

the how-to: filling

In a small saucepan, heat the cream over medium-low heat until just barely simmering (not boiling!). Turn off the heat and add the chocolate chips. Let the mixture sit for 5 to 8 minutes, then stir until smooth. Set it aside to cool until thick but spreadable.

the how-to: buttercream

1 In a medium saucepan (with the heat off!), whisk together the granulated sugar, cornstarch, cocoa powder, and salt. Add the eggs one at a time, whisking thoroughly between each addition. Slowly pour in the milk, whisking constantly. Turn on the heat to medium and whisk constantly until the mixture starts to bubble. Once bubbling, continue whisking for about 1 minute, until very thick, then immediately remove it from the heat. Scrape the custard into the bowl of your electric mixer and put it in the fridge to cool completely, 30 to 45 minutes.

2 Once cool, beat the custard in your stand mixer using the whisk attachment on medium-high speed for 2 minutes. With the machine running, add the butter a couple of tablespoons at a time. Add the vanilla extract and beat to combine. Continue whipping on medium-high speed for about 4 minutes, until very, very fluffy.

the how-to: assembly

Set the first cake layer on a serving platter. Add half of the filling to the top of the cake and, using an offset spatula, spread it out into an even layer. Stack the second layer on top and repeat with the second half of the filling. Stack the third layer on top. Frost the sides and top of the cake with the buttercream. Store in the fridge, covered, for up to 5 days.

note: If you are a raspberry and chocolate type of person, you can add 2 tablespoons Framboise liqueur to the filling after you melt the chocolate. I am *not* a raspberry and chocolate type of person, but I tried it out for you anyway and even I liked it.

YOU MIGHT BE FEELING:
*sensitive, up and down, ready to
go home to your fluffy slippers*

Raise your hand if you've ever been called "moody" for simply expressing your feelings. My hand is raised, and maybe yours is too! Brushing off complex emotions as moodiness is an old and tired strategy for dismissing someone's feelings—and this is especially true if you happen to be a woman. So instead, let's talk about how wonderful and important it is to experience and explore your feelings, for the following (and many more) reasons:

It enables you to be in tune with the people you love, and support them through their highs and lows.

It gives you permission to take space for yourself if you need it.

It helps cultivate your capacity for empathy and compassion.

It gives you insight into what you want/don't want, and what you need/don't need.

So: let's be gentle with ourselves and spend some time making really good cookies.

thick & chewy maple cookies

MAKES A BAKER'S DOZEN (13 COOKIES!)

These are *thick* cookies. They're soft and chewy, with a slight crunch on the edges from a brown sugar coating. At first glance, maple and cayenne might seem like a strange flavor combo, but I promise it's delicious. Think of the warmth of a gingerbread cookie, with the sweetness of pancakes drenched in syrup. They're not actually spicy—you'll just detect a little heat on the back of your tongue after the second bite! I'm going to let you in on a (little? big?) secret: this is my favorite recipe in the book.

This recipe is the cookie version of a warm and comforting hug from someone who loves you (in all of your moods). Instead of focusing on managing or judging yourself for your current mood, try focusing on the sweet heat of the cayenne and maple when you sample one of these. I *strongly* recommend grabbing a taste while they're still warm.

FOR THE COOKIES

2½ cups (325g) all-purpose flour

1 teaspoon baking soda

¾ teaspoon kosher salt

¼ teaspoon cayenne pepper

1 cup (2 sticks, 227g) room temp unsalted butter

1 cup (200g) light brown sugar

1 large egg

1 large egg yolk

2 teaspoons maple extract

½ teaspoon vanilla extract

½ cup (100g) light brown sugar, for rolling

the how-to

1 Preheat the oven to 350°F and line a baking sheet with parchment paper.

2 In a medium bowl, whisk together the flour, baking soda, salt, and cayenne pepper.

3 In the bowl of a stand mixer, cream together the butter and brown sugar on medium-high speed until creamy, about 2 minutes. Beat in the egg, egg yolk, maple extract, and vanilla extract. Turn off the mixer and add the flour mixture. Mix on low speed until the dough comes together.

4 Form the dough into 3-tablespoon (60g) balls. Roll each ball in brown sugar, completely covering all of the surfaces.

5 Place the cookies at least 3 inches apart on the baking sheet. Bake for 12 to 14 minutes, until golden around the edges but soft in the middle. Let the cookies cool on the pan for 2 minutes, then transfer them to a wire rack. Store in an airtight container out on the counter for up to 4 days.

note: The trick to these cookies is to slightly underbake them. We want that ooey gooey center! Trust me!

SELFISH
~~~~~~~~~~

YOU MIGHT BE FEELING:
*like you don't have the capacity
to consider other people's
wants or needs today*
~~~~~~~~~~

First of all, OK—you've recognized you're "being selfish." There's no need to repeat it on loop while we're baking today! Let's take a break from the thought by engaging with your senses and doing something with your hands.

Sometimes when we're feeling selfish in the moment, we extrapolate that feeling into a critique of our character—"I'm a selfish *person*." But these are not the same things! You can be a kind, compassionate, caring person and still experience selfishness, jealousy, and other emotions that we often judge harshly. Many times when we're telling ourselves that we're "selfish," we're actually tuning in to our wants and needs. There's an irony here, because when we regularly deny our own needs, prioritizing ourselves can make us feel worse than not caring for ourselves. So maybe this emotion is showing up here as an opportunity to reframe your thinking: your needs matter too.

rainbow cookie cake

MAKES A 9-INCH COOKIE CAKE

Does cookie cake remind you of that birthday party at Chuck E. Cheese for your friend Shelby in second grade? Just me? Anyway—in my opinion, cookie cake is the best of both worlds. It has the fanciness of a cake, with the unfussiness of a cookie. This one is the standard chocolate chip cookie base, but we're going to dress it up with a dash of rainbow sprinkles and a smidge of brown sugar Swiss buttercream on the top. It's going to be great, and while a cookie cake is super easy to share, you can definitely keep the whole thing for yourself, if that's what you want to do today.

FOR THE COOKIE CAKE

2 cups (260g) all-purpose flour

1 teaspoon baking soda

1 teaspoon kosher salt

¾ cup (1½ sticks, 170g) room temp unsalted butter

¾ cup (150g) dark brown sugar

¼ cup (50g) granulated sugar

1 large egg

1 large egg yolk

2 teaspoons vanilla extract

1¼ cups (219g) semisweet chocolate chips

¼ cup rainbow sprinkles + more for topping

FOR THE BROWN SUGAR SWISS BUTTERCREAM

1 large egg white

¼ cup (50g) dark brown sugar

6 tablespoons (85g) cool room temp unsalted butter

¼ teaspoon vanilla extract

food coloring (optional!): I like pink, but the
color's up to you, friend!

the how-to: cookie cake

1 Grease the bottom and sides of a 9-inch
cake pan.

2 In a medium bowl, whisk together the flour,
baking soda, and salt.

3 In the bowl of a stand mixer fitted with the
paddle attachment, cream together the
butter, brown sugar, and granulated sugar
on medium-high speed until fluffy, about
2 minutes. Scrape down the bottom and
sides of the bowl with a rubber spatula.
Beat in the egg, egg yolk, and vanilla
extract on medium speed until thoroughly
incorporated. Add the flour mixture all at
once and mix on low speed until combined.
Add the chocolate chips and sprinkles
and mix on low speed just until evenly
distributed. Give the dough a good stir with
a rubber spatula or wooden spoon to make
sure everything's mixed in well.

4 Plop the dough into your prepared cake
pan and smooth it around into an even
layer. Bake for 28 to 32 minutes, until
deeply golden and a tester inserted comes
out clean. Let cool completely on a wire
rack before decorating.

the how-to: buttercream

1 While the cake is cooling, make your
buttercream! Heat a large pot of water
over medium heat until simmering. Whisk
together the egg white and brown sugar
in a heatproof metal bowl (it should be
slightly larger than the pot). Wearing an
oven mitt, carefully place the bowl over the
simmering water (making sure the water
doesn't actually touch the bowl). Keep
whisking until you can't feel the sugar if
you rub it (carefully! It's hot!) between your
fingertips, 2 to 3 minutes.

2 Transfer the hot egg white mixture to the
bowl of a stand mixer. Using the whisk
attachment, beat on medium-high speed
until mixture doubles in size, turns glossy,
and soft peaks form, about 5 minutes.

3 Add the butter, 2 tablespoons at a time.
Continue whipping on medium-high speed
until very fluffy, about 5 minutes. Beat in
the vanilla extract and add food coloring (if
you like!).

4 Transfer the frosting to a piping bag fitted
with any piping tip you'd like (or a plastic
bag with the end cut off!) and decorate.
I like to pipe star shapes around the sides
and write a cute lil' message in the center.
Top with more sprinkles. Store at room
temperature for up to 2 days.

Remember when I prompted you to write down the feelings that you revisit often (on page 11)? Well, this is one of mine! I've been told many times that I'm too strong-willed for my own good. So I want to start off by saying that there's nothing inherently wrong with feeling stubborn, despite the messaging you might have received growing up. It can help you stand up for yourself (or someone else) and hold your ground when you need to. Sometimes I'm quite proud of my stubbornness. And other times I feel trapped in it. So it might be useful to take a minute and explore how you're feeling *about* the stubborn feeling in order to process it. There's no one-size-fits-all approach to feelings, and it's OK to loosen your grip on your stubbornness if that serves you today. Despite what my brain likes to tell me, it doesn't mean you're losing or failing!

blueberry almond coffee cake

MAKES A 9 X 13-INCH CAKE

Unlike us humans who can often be stubbornly set in our ways, there's a lot of variability with coffee cakes. Do they contain cinnamon, or not? Are they dense or fluffy? But, thankfully, they almost always feature a crumb topping (we love a good crumb topping). Because we're using cake flour instead of all-purpose, this recipe makes a very light and fluffy cake, with no cinnamon in sight. We're baking it in a 9 x 13-inch pan, so this recipe makes *a lot* of coffee cake. You'll be all set for both breakfast and after-dinner snacks for the week.

Now: Does your oven have a little window with a light you can turn on? If so, check in on the cake every so often. Notice how it's changed since the last time you looked. Is the crumble turning golden? Is the juice from the blueberries bubbling? Watch the way it springs up in the pan. The point is—even if you don't notice it, change is always happening!

*Important note: If your oven does not have a little window, don't open the oven door! You don't want to let any of the heat out—you could end up with a deflated cake.

FOR THE CRUMB TOPPING

¾ cup (98g) all-purpose flour
⅔ cup (133g) light brown sugar
½ cup (50g) sliced almonds
a pinch of kosher salt
6 tablespoons (85g) melted unsalted butter

3½ cups (455g) + 1 tablespoon cake flour,
 divided

1 tablespoon baking powder

1 teaspoon kosher salt

1 cup whole milk

¾ cup (180g) sour cream

1 cup (2 sticks, 227g) room temp unsalted butter

¾ cup (150g) granulated sugar

½ cup (100g) light brown sugar

3 large eggs

2 teaspoons vanilla extract

½ teaspoon almond extract

1 cup (about 170g) blueberries, fresh or frozen

the how-to: crumb topping

1 Preheat the oven to 350°F. Line a 9 x 13-inch pan with a strip of parchment paper. Grease the parchment paper and exposed sides.

2 In a small bowl, stir together all of the crumb topping ingredients using a fork. Set aside until later.

the how-to: cake

1 In a medium bowl, whisk together 3½ cups (455g) of the cake flour, the baking powder, and salt. In a glass measuring cup or small bowl, stir together the milk and sour cream with a fork until smooth.

2 In the bowl of a stand mixer fitted with the paddle attachment, cream together the butter, granulated sugar, and brown sugar on medium-high speed until very light and fluffy, about 3 minutes. Scrape down the sides and bottom of the bowl. Beat in the eggs on medium-high speed, one at a time, until completely incorporated. Add

the vanilla extract and almond extract. Scrape down the sides and bottom of the bowl again. With the mixer running on low, add in the flour mixture and milk mixture in three alternating batches, starting and ending with the flour mixture.

3 In a small bowl, stir together the blueberries and the remaining 1 tablespoon cake flour. Using a rubber spatula, gently fold the blueberries into the batter by hand. Spread the batter into your prepared pan and smooth the top with an offset spatula. Top evenly with the crumb topping.

4 Bake for 45 to 50 minutes, until the cake looks golden brown and a tester inserted in the center comes out clean. Set on a wire rack to cool completely. Store at room temp in an airtight container for up to 3 days.

I'm so sorry that someone did you wrong. And I'm positive that you don't deserve it. Also: I'm glad you know what you deserve, and recognize that you didn't get it. Wanting revenge is super common! I'm pretty sure it serves as the plotline in 75 percent of thriller movies. Vengeful is, by definition, a past-focused feeling. So let's spend some time dreaming about the future.

Here's what I want you to do:

Spend the next five-ish minutes writing down everything that you want from your life. This can be anything! Places you want to visit, the chosen family you want to build, feelings you want to experience, contributions you want to make, foods you want to try. Maybe you want to live in a house on a cliff next to the sea. Maybe you want to invent something that no one's ever thought of. Maybe you want to host huge holiday dinners with your approximately sixteen grandchildren. Maybe you want to learn how to make wine or win a spicy pepper eating contest.

Maybe you want all of these things, or none of them! Whatever it is you hope for, take some time to envision all the wonderful things you completely deserve.

black pepper snowballs

MAKES ABOUT 36 COOKIES

I know you might be skeptical about the pepper. In fact, adding black pepper to cookies might even sound like a form of revenge! But just suspend your doubt and trust me for an hour—I promise you it works. These are a variation of the traditional holiday cookie—full of ground nuts and completely covered in powdered sugar. They have a deep, sweet, satisfying flavor from the toasted walnuts, dark brown sugar, and a healthy pinch of freshly ground black pepper. You mix the cookie dough with your hands (yay). And please note: It does not have to be a holiday for you to make and enjoy these cookies.

Dousing things in powdered sugar is a great activity when you're incandescent with thoughts of revenge. There's something really cathartic about being able to visualize the furious feeling flying all around you.

FOR THE COOKIES

1½ cups (175g) toasted walnuts

¼ cup (50g) dark brown sugar

½ teaspoon freshly ground black pepper

½ teaspoon fresh lemon zest

a pinch of ground nutmeg

a pinch of kosher salt

1 cup (130g) all-purpose flour

1 teaspoon vanilla extract

½ cup (1 stick, 113g) room temp unsalted butter, cut into ½ inch pieces

MAD

1 cup (120g) powdered sugar, for rolling

the how-to

1 Preheat the oven to 350°F and line a baking sheet with parchment paper.

2 In the bowl of a food processor, pulse the walnuts, brown sugar, black pepper, lemon zest, nutmeg, and salt until finely ground.

3 In a medium bowl, whisk together the nut mixture and flour. Add the vanilla extract and butter pieces. Using your hands, mix until a dough is formed.

4 Roll into 1-inch (pretty tiny!) balls. Bake for 14 to 15 minutes, until set and slightly golden.

5 As soon as the cookies are cool enough to handle, gently roll them in the powdered sugar. Transfer to a wire rack. When the cookies have cooled completely, shower them in more powdered sugar. Store at room temp in an airtight container for up to 5 days.

anxious

The recipes in this chapter are here to help you figure out and get friendly with what's bothering you.

Vibes: A sinking feeling in your stomach, accidentally getting off at the wrong bus stop, waking up suddenly at 5:52 a.m. when you don't actually have to be up 'til 7:15

Anxiety can feel all-consuming. If you're someone who experiences anxious feelings, it's likely that at some point, a well-meaning person in your life has attempted to reassure you by saying something like: "Everything's fine. There's nothing to worry about!" I've definitely heard that one before, and I'm here to validate what you already know: there is no way to simply *think* your way out of anxiety. And in fact, it takes a good amount of effort, not to mention bravery, to work through these feelings.

Instead of trying to conquer anxiety, let's explore and acknowledge these feelings, and then let them go. I like to close my eyes and picture myself gently floating down a calm river in an inner tube on a warm and sunny summer day. The cool water balances out the warmth of the sun on my skin. There are lots of things to look at—big puffy clouds, sunlight streaming through green leaves, birds flying above, the glimmer of the water. You can count on the slow and steady pace of the water, floating on to the next thing to see. Channel this slow, steady introspection when getting in touch with your feelings—really study them, instead of keeping them

at an arm's length. Notice where your mind wanders. Notice how your body feels.

We're often told to "feel our feelings." But if you're anything like me, when you hear that you might think, "OK, but what does that actually *mean*, and *how* do I do it?" For a long time, I thought it meant I had to hyper-focus my brain on the emotion—like, if I just thought hard enough about being worried, that would be feeling it. But it turns out that it's more about your body than your brain! Speaking of, the "flavors of anxious" feelings tend to announce themselves loudly in my body. They might show up as a sinking nauseous feeling in my stomach, a cold prickling across my chest, a tingling in my hands, or, most frequently in my case, a migraine. Take a second to check in with your body and see if you notice if any of your feelings are showing up there. If you identify a sensation—great job for noticing it. If you don't detect anything right now, that's OK too. If you did identify a sensation, let's take a second to greet it rather than try to banish it. Give the sensation space. Try not to judge or change it. For a minute, let your body rather than your mind do the processing.

FLAVORS OF

anxious

confused

embarrassed

impatient

overwhelmed

lost

panicked

scared

scattered

restless

sorry

worried

trapped

stressed

CONFUSED

~~~

YOU MIGHT BE FEELING:

*like the ground is unsteady
beneath you; as though
life's a giant math problem
you can't seem to solve*

~~~

Sometimes there's not a clear path ahead of us, and that can feel uncomfortable or scary. But, the beautiful thing about life is that there's not just one path. There are many, all with differently wonderful moments and differently challenging outcomes. I actually find a lot of comfort in this idea. After all, if there's not a set path, you don't have to worry about deviating from it. You can give yourself permission to explore.

If you've ever lost a job, you're intimately familiar with the disorienting feeling of not knowing what comes next—like you missed a step. I got laid off right before the COVID-19 pandemic. I spent the next several months applying for job after job, doing interview after interview, but not being able to find one. It was a very unsettling time, but somewhere amid all that confusion and self-doubt and frustration, I decided to write this book! I slowly let go of my tight grip on the idea that if I didn't have a certain type of job, I was a failure. Confusion often comes at the beginning of starting something new. So consider that it might be a sign that you're growing! It's OK to change directions. It's OK to trust and bet on yourself.

vanilla chocolate twist cookies

MAKES ABOUT 18 COOKIES

This cookie is perfect for the days when it feels impossible to make decisions, big or small. Small, as in: Do I want a chocolate cookie or a sugar cookie? Don't worry, I've got this one—we're going to make both!

These are medium-sized cookies with a chewy center and crisp edges. The beauty of them is that you get two distinct and yummy flavors: the vanilla half and the chocolate half. There are several ways of eating them: eat the whole vanilla side first, eat the whole chocolate side first, work your way around in an even pattern taking bites from each, or fold it in half like a cookie sandwich so you get even bites of each. Every path to the finish line here is a delicious one.

FOR THE COOKIE DOUGH

2 cups (260g) all-purpose flour

¾ teaspoon baking soda

½ teaspoon kosher salt

1 cup (2 sticks, 227g) room temp unsalted butter

1¼ cups (250g) granulated sugar

¼ cup (50g) light brown sugar

1 large egg

2 teaspoons vanilla extract

2 tablespoons Dutch-process cocoa powder

FOR THE COATING

½ cup (100g) granulated sugar

the how-to: cookie dough

1 Preheat the oven to 350°F and line a baking sheet with parchment paper.

2 In a medium bowl, whisk together the flour, baking soda, and salt.

3 In the bowl of a stand mixer fitted with the paddle attachment, cream together the butter, granulated sugar, and brown sugar on medium-high speed until creamy, about 2 minutes. Scrape down the sides of the bowl. Beat in the egg and vanilla extract on medium speed until thoroughly combined. Scrape down the sides of the bowl again. Add the flour mixture all at once and mix on low speed until the dough comes together.

4 Remove half of the dough from the mixer and set it aside—this will be your vanilla half. If you want to be very sure that your halves are even you can measure using your kitchen scale, but usually I just eyeball it! Add the cocoa powder to the mixer bowl and stir until it just incorporates into the dough.

the how-to: assembly & coating

Using 1 tablespoon of vanilla dough and 1 tablespoon of chocolate dough for each, lightly squish the pieces together and form the dough into 2-tablespoon (40g) sized balls. Roll each ball in the granulated sugar, completely covering all of the surfaces. Place the cookies at least 3 inches apart on the baking sheet. Bake for 11 to 13 minutes, until crisp around the edges and just set in the middle. Let the cookies cool on the sheet for 2 minutes, then transfer them to a wire rack. Store at room temp in an airtight container for up to 2 days.

Ah, embarrassment. As someone who once peed my pants in the elementary school computer lab, I know it's an uncomfortable feeling. OK, actually that's a secondhand story from someone I love who shall remain nameless, but the imagery, wow! You didn't think I'd share my *actual* most embarrassing story, did you? It's way too embarrassing for that!

There's a whole spectrum of embarrassment—from calling your teacher "Mom" in front of the whole class, all the way to painful and long-lasting humiliation. Minor forms can help you laugh at yourself, and maybe let go of a little bit of pride that's not really serving you. But as we all know, embarrassment isn't always minor. It can run quite deep, entwined with feelings of vulnerability and shame.

And ghosts of these intense moments of embarrassment (big and small) can persist for years, showing up at inopportune times, perhaps while you're cozy in bed trying to fall asleep! So, let's remember this: everyone has their own moments of embarrassment that are specific to their stories and values. While the moments are different for everyone, you are absolutely not alone in this feeling. And your cheeks can't stay red forever.

pumpkin pie bars

MAKES 9 LARGE-ISH BARS

This recipe takes the fussiness out of making pumpkin pie while maintaining its special occasion vibe. And good news for timing/ease: we're not making pie crust! The bars are three layers: a shortbread crust, a spiced pumpkin filling, and a sour cream topping. Each is delicious in its own right, but they're especially good as a trio. You typically find sour cream topping on cheesecake, but I find that it works well here as a slightly tangy counterweight to the warming flavor of the pumpkin filling.

I find eating one of these straight out of the fridge can cool down even the harshest of heats of humiliation. And yes, it's fine to eat pumpkin pie outside of November—it's nothing to be embarrassed about ;)

FOR THE SHORTBREAD CRUST

1¼ cups (163g) all-purpose flour

¼ cup (50g) granulated sugar

¼ teaspoon kosher salt

½ cup (1 stick, 113g) melted unsalted butter

FOR THE SOUR CREAM TOPPING

1 cup (240g) sour cream

2 tablespoons granulated sugar

¼ teaspoon vanilla extract

FOR THE FILLING

One 15-oz (425g) can pumpkin puree

⅔ cup (133g) dark brown sugar

¾ teaspoon kosher salt

1½ teaspoons ground cinnamon

½ teaspoon ground ginger

⅛ teaspoon ground cardamom

⅛ teaspoon ground cloves

⅛ teaspoon freshly ground black pepper

a pinch of ground nutmeg

1¼ cups cold heavy cream

3 large eggs

the how-to: shortbread crust

1 Preheat the oven to 350°F. Line the bottom and two sides of an 8-inch square cake pan with an overhanging strip of parchment paper cut to the width of the bottom of the pan. Grease the exposed sides of the pan.

2 In a medium bowl, whisk together the flour, granulated sugar, and salt. Add the melted butter and stir with a rubber spatula until the dough comes together. Add the dough to your prepared pan, and press it down evenly using your fingertips. Bake the crust for 15 to 17 minutes, until it's just lightly golden around the edges. Set aside on a wire rack to cool.

the how-to: sour cream topping

Stir together the sour cream, granulated sugar, and vanilla extract in a glass measuring cup or small bowl. Set aside for later.

the how-to: filling

1 In a medium saucepan, stir together the pumpkin puree, brown sugar, salt, cinnamon, ginger, cardamom, cloves, black pepper, and nutmeg. Bring to a simmer, and cook over medium heat, stirring, for 5 minutes. This step cooks out some of the moisture in the pumpkin and ensures a silky final product. Transfer the mixture to a large bowl. Whisk in the heavy cream until smooth. Add the eggs one at a time, whisking thoroughly between each addition. Pour the mixture over your baked shortbread crust.

2 Bake the bars for 40 to 44 minutes, until the edges are set but the center is still jiggly. Remove the bars from the oven. Add the sour cream topping and gently smooth it around to the edges. Put the bars back in the oven and bake for another 10 minutes.

3 Set the bars on a wire rack to cool completely in the pan, then lift them out using the parchment paper sling to slice and serve. I prefer these cold from the fridge, but they can also be served at room temperature. Store in the fridge, covered, for up to 4 days.

I somehow happen to be married to the most patient person in the world, I'm pretty sure. I'm always in awe of his ability to stay cool, because boy do I not relate. But after all these years of being impatient, one thing I've learned is that focusing on how incredibly slow time is moving (unfortunately) doesn't make it move any faster. So: let's exercise those patience muscles by waiting for some dough to rise (multiple times!). Yes, it's definitely a *little* tedious, but this recipe is here to help you exist in this moment and go with the flow. And might I suggest grabbing some headphones and putting on an episode (or three) of your fave podcast while you wait? Get lost in the story! Try not to check your email!

pecan morning buns

MAKES 12 BUNS

Despite being a giant hunk of pastry, morning buns are just so *cute*. These have a sweet (but not overly sweet!) and creamy pecan filling—think frangipane, but no almonds—rolled in, plus the satisfying crunch of little pecan pieces scattered throughout. And: a warm and toasty bourbon-spiked butterscotch-like glaze on the top.

Here, I want you to focus in on the (admittedly, rather lengthy) process. Let yourself enjoy it, rather than just complete it. Pay attention to the way the dough springs back against your finger when you test to see if it's ready to move on to the next step. Breathe in the sweet, rich scent of the frangipane as you spread it across the dough. Notice the way the floss feels as it slices through the dough spiral. Turn on some music. Get lost in the process.

note: Like in the Coffee Glazed Cinnamon Rolls (page 81) recipe, you'll need dental floss for this recipe. Unflavored is best, but mint is fine!

FOR THE DOUGH

1 cup whole milk

½ cup (1 stick, 113g) unsalted butter, cut into ½-inch slices

4½ cups (585g) all-purpose flour + more if needed

½ cup (100g) granulated sugar

2¼ teaspoons (7g, 1 standard packet) active dry yeast

1 teaspoon kosher salt

2 large room temp eggs

a couple teaspoons vegetable oil to coat the bowl

FOR THE FILLING, PART 1

½ cup (60g) toasted pecans

½ cup (100g) dark brown sugar

1 large egg

4 tablespoons (½ stick 57g) room temp
    unsalted butter

1 tablespoon all-purpose flour

a pinch of ground nutmeg

a pinch of kosher salt

1 teaspoon vanilla extract

FOR THE FILLING, PART 2

½ cup (60g) toasted and coarsely
    chopped pecans

⅓ cup (67g) granulated sugar

FOR THE GLAZE

¾ cup (150g) dark brown sugar

¼ cup water

3 tablespoons (42g) unsalted butter

a pinch of kosher salt

1 teaspoon vanilla extract

1 tablespoon bourbon (optional)

1 cup (120g) powdered sugar

the how-to: dough

1 In a glass measuring cup (or medium heatproof bowl), combine the milk and butter. Microwave in 30-second increments, stirring in between, until the butter is just melted. Set aside to cool to lukewarm temperature.

2 In the bowl of a stand mixer fitted with the dough hook attachment, combine the flour, granulated sugar, yeast, and salt.

3 Add the eggs to the lukewarm milk/butter mixture and whisk with a fork to combine.

Pour the wet ingredient mixture into the dry ingredient mixture. Knead the mixture with the dough hook for 8 to 9 minutes, until it feels slightly sticky but smooth. If your dough feels too wet, add another tablespoon or two of flour. Scrape the dough out onto a lightly floured surface and lightly coat the bowl in vegetable oil. Return the dough to the bowl and cover it with plastic wrap. Let rise out on the counter for 1½ to 2 hours (depending on how warm your kitchen is), until nearly doubled in size. If you press your finger lightly into the dough, it should spring back.

the how-to: filling

1 While the dough is rising, make your filling. Place the pecans and brown sugar in the work bowl of a food processor and process until finely ground. Add the egg and run the food processor until combined. Add the butter, flour, nutmeg, salt, and vanilla extract and process until smooth. Set aside until needed.

2 Once the dough has risen, turn it out onto a lightly floured surface. Roll it out into a 12 x 18-inch rectangle. Coat the rectangle evenly with the pecan mixture, leaving a ½-inch border on each side. Scatter the remaining pecan pieces and granulated sugar evenly over the top. Starting on a long edge, roll the dough up into a tight cylinder. Pinch the seam to seal. Using dental floss, cut the cylinder into 12 equal sections. I do this by dividing it in half, dividing the two sections in half, and then dividing the four sections into three. It will be a little messy—don't worry too much if some of the filling escapes.

3   Grease a standard 12-well muffin tin. Place a bun into each well. Cover the pan loosely with plastic wrap and set out on the counter to rise for another 30 to 60 minutes, until the buns are slightly puffed. While the buns are rising, preheat the oven to 350°F.

4   Bake for 30 to 33 minutes, until lightly golden brown on the top.

the how-to: glaze

As soon as you take the buns out of the oven, make your glaze! In a small pot, combine the brown sugar and water. Bring to a simmer over medium-low heat and cook until the sugar dissolves, 2 to 3 minutes. Whisk in the butter. Turn off the heat. Whisk in the salt, vanilla extract, bourbon (if using), and powdered sugar until smooth. Pop the buns out of the pan and place them on a wire cooling rack set on top of a sheet pan (to catch any drips!). Spoon the glaze evenly over the warm buns.

note: If you want to make this an overnight recipe instead, put the plastic wrap–covered muffin tin of cut buns into the fridge overnight. In the morning, put them out on the counter for 1 to 1½ hours until they look puffy, then proceed to the baking.

YOU MIGHT BE FEELING:
*drained, weary, out
of fucks to give*

To me *overwhelmed* is a big and often visceral feeling. Sometimes it feels like a tingling in my chest, sometimes like a creeping flush in my face, sometimes like shallow breaths. And feeling overwhelmed is usually the tip of a very large iceberg that includes other things like: a lack of support/resources, an inability to take the time to really care for myself, or spreading myself so thin I practically disappear.

Sometimes we're buzzing around so much that we don't even notice that we're overwhelmed until everything comes crashing down. So, let's take a minute to acknowledge some of the things that might be contributing to feeling overwhelmed. Get out your notebook and make a list! There's no need to edit your thoughts here—no one's watching.

coconut no bakes

MAKES ABOUT 20 NO-BAKE COOKIES

When I'm feeling overwhelmed, I like to go after the easy wins. So today we're going to make cookies without even turning on the oven. This recipe is great for those times when your inner monologue sounds something like *How the fuck does anyone do all of this? And how do they make it look so easy?* It's also great for those times when you need to bring a dessert somewhere and you have exactly fifteen minutes to figure it out. It takes only a little bit of effort, but you get a lot of reward. The only difficult part is waiting for the cookies to cool (but if you get impatient, the dough tastes great right off a spoon).

4 tablespoons (½ stick, 57g) unsalted butter

¾ cup (150g) light brown sugar

¼ cup milk (I use whole, but any type is OK—
   oat, almond, soy, etc.)

2 tablespoons unsweetened cocoa powder

⅛ teaspoon ground cinnamon

a pinch of kosher salt

1 teaspoon vanilla extract

½ cup (35g) sweetened coconut flakes

1 cup (100g) old-fashioned oats

OPTIONAL (BUT HIGHLY RECOMMENDED) TOPPINGS

2 tablespoons melted creamy peanut butter (not natural)

sweetened coconut flakes, for sprinkling

flaky salt (such as Maldon), for sprinkling

the how-to

In a medium saucepan, melt the butter over medium heat. Whisk in the brown sugar, milk, cocoa powder, cinnamon, and kosher salt. Bring to a simmer over medium heat and cook, stirring, for 2 minutes. Remove from the heat and stir in the vanilla extract. Stir in the shredded coconut and oats. Let cool for about 5 minutes. Scoop into 1-tablespoon (20g) sized balls onto parchment paper. Optional: drizzle with the melted peanut butter and sprinkle with the coconut flakes/flaky salt. Let sit until set, about 20 minutes. Store in the fridge, covered, for up to a week.

YOU MIGHT BE FEELING:
*adrift, confused, unsure
of what to do next*

Even though it's impossible to know exactly where we're going, it's difficult to let go and trust the messy journey—especially when other people's lives seem to be unfolding just as planned.

But here's a silver lining to feeling lost: it's a pretty great opportunity to explore. Maybe this is the moment to shift course, to meet someone new, to go somewhere you've never been, to consider possibilities you've never considered. Your path can be built one step at a time. You can redraw your map as many times as you want. No matter how uncertain you feel at this moment, you have the power to recalibrate from here. You don't have to have it all figured out!

becca's brownies

MAKES 9 LARGE-ISH BROWNIES

Growing up, I ate a lot of boxed brownies. The gooey center, chewy edges, and crackly top are deeply ingrained in my childhood memories. So I want to be very clear that there's nothing wrong with a boxed mix. But if you can get that boxed brownie effect without having to put on pants to go to the store . . . why not go for it?

I like to make these when I'm craving something comfortable, familiar, and grounding. There's nothing that'll bring your wandering mind back home faster than a homemade brownie. Pro tip: store them in the fridge and eat 'em cold.

1 cup (175g) semisweet chocolate chips
½ cup (1 stick, 113g) unsalted butter, cut into lil' bits
1½ teaspoons vanilla extract
⅓ cup (45g) all-purpose flour
¼ cup (25g) unsweetened cocoa powder
½ teaspoon kosher salt
¼ teaspoon ground cinnamon
1 cup (200g) granulated sugar
2 large eggs

the how-to

1 Preheat the oven to 350°F and line the bottom and sides of an 8-inch square baking pan with parchment paper. Grease the parchment paper.

2 Put the chocolate chips and butter in a medium heatproof bowl. Microwave in 30-second increments until melted, stirring between each increment. Watch carefully to make sure you don't burn your chocolate! Stir in the vanilla extract. Set aside to cool slightly.

ANXIOUS

3   In a small bowl, whisk together the flour, cocoa powder, salt, and cinnamon.

4   In a large bowl, whisk together the sugar and eggs for a minute or two, until the mixture is thick and pale yellow. Whisk in the chocolate mixture. Fold in the dry ingredients with a rubber spatula.

5   Pour the batter into your prepared pan— it will be thick! Make sure to spread it out all the way to the edges of the pan in an even layer. Bake for 30 minutes, or until set. Let cool completely (yes, really). Store at room temp in an airtight container for up to 3 days.

notes: Don't try to cut the brownies until they're cool! Really —you'll end up with a gooey mess (a delicious mess, but just trust me). You can hurry things along by putting the pan in the freezer.

Yes, you can omit the cinnamon if you must (break my heart).

I don't know about you, but when I feel panicked my head starts swirling with unhelpful thoughts, such as: "You don't need to worry so much," or "There's nothing to be scared of," or maybe even "Why do you stress out about such stupid things when everyone else seems so confident all the time?" What if instead of dismissing the feeling or covering it up, you listened to what is has to say?

Let your fears be heard. Let them know that you've heard them. And then challenge the ways your brain is trying to catastrophize those fears into a full-on imminent crisis. Consider that working to find a solution to this one particular problem in this one particular moment is enough.

salty brown butter caramels

MAKES ABOUT 64 CARAMELS

Are you a candy person? I am. I used to dig around in my grandma's purse in search of those seemingly unique to the '90s gold foil–wrapped butterscotch hard candies. But I've learned how to make my own, and now, I definitely prefer a buttery, chewy, melt-in-your-mouth caramel to a hard candy (but I mean, it's not like I'd say *no* to a Werther's). All candy making requires precision, but there's no need to panic—this recipe isn't complicated (really!). And in fact, making candy is a great activity when you're feeling overwhelmed *because* it requires you to slow down and pay attention. If you're intently watching the candy thermometer for the exact moment when your caramel reaches 248°F, your brain has something to focus on besides a swirling, catastrophizing thought process.

*note: You (really) need a candy thermometer for this one! Also, I won't typically ask you to buy fancy butter, but if you've got some Plugra lying around, now's the time to use it!

4 tablespoons (½ stick, 57g) unsalted butter

1 cup + 2 tablespoons heavy cream (fussy, but necessary)

2 teaspoons flaky salt (such as Maldon) + more for sprinkling

¼ teaspoon ground cinnamon

1 cup (200g) granulated sugar

½ cup (100g) light brown sugar

¼ cup light corn syrup

¼ cup water

1 teaspoon vanilla extract

just a tiny bit of vegetable oil (to coat the knife when you're cutting your cooled caramels)

the how-to:

1 Line the bottom and sides of an 8-inch square pan with two crisscrossing lengths of parchment paper.

2 Heat a medium pot over medium heat. Add the butter and heat until it's melted, brown, and nutty, stirring often. Watch it carefully, and turn off the heat as soon as it reaches a deep caramel color. Add the cream, flaky salt, and cinnamon and stir to combine. Set aside for a bit.

3 Clip a candy thermometer to the side of a large heavy-bottomed pot (I use a Dutch oven). Add the granulated sugar, brown sugar, corn syrup, and water. Stir with a rubber spatula to combine into a thick paste, and then set that spatula down! Boil over medium heat—don't stir—until the mixture reaches 300°F (this will take a while, but it will get there). Immediately remove it from the heat, then slowly pour in the butter mixture and stir with a rubber spatula to combine. Turn the heat back on to medium-high and boil (without stirring!) until the caramel reaches 248°F. Immediately remove the caramel from the heat and stir in the vanilla extract.

4 Pour the caramel into your prepared pan set on top of a wire rack to cool until firm, about 2 hours out on the counter or 1 hour in the fridge.

5 While you're waiting, cut out your wax paper squares. You'll need about seventy 3-inch squares (technically 64, but it's always good to have extra).

6 When the caramels are cool, lift them out using the parchment paper sling and transfer to a cutting board to slice. Top with more flaky salt to taste. Using a sharp knife (or bench scraper) coated in vegetable oil, cut the caramels into 1-inch squares. If your knife starts sticking, coat it in more vegetable oil.

7 Wrap each caramel in a wax paper square and twist the sides to seal. Serve at room temp or cold from the fridge. Store at room temp in an airtight container for up to 2 weeks, or in the fridge for up to a month.

note: Feel free to cut the caramels into different shapes/ sizes! It's definitely a personal preference type of thing.

YOU MIGHT BE FEELING:
*unsettled, riled up, ready to
get a move on (even if you're
not sure where you're going)*

Right now, you might be feeling like you want to be somewhere else, but maybe you're not sure exactly where. It's a feeling of being "in between," or pulled in several directions. I think of restlessness as a future-focused emotion. And since we obviously/unfortunately can't predict the future, it can be unsettling. But: if you're feeling restless, you might also be feeling excited and open to change/new possibilities! Maybe you can reframe the restlessness in a more positive light, as a beautiful willingness to expand and explore your world.

And in the meantime, let's do a quick exercise courtesy of a lovely teacher from my yoga class era (circa 2015–2017). Take a seat—I like sitting cross-legged on the floor, but whatever's comfortable for you is just fine. Place the palms of your hands on the tops of your thighs, facing down. Softly close your eyes. Take a deep breath in through your nose, then out through your nose. Feel the steadiness of the earth/ground/chair beneath you. Notice the subtle weight of your palms. Let the rhythm of your breath—slowly in through your nose, slowly out through your nose—ground you in this moment. When you feel ready, open your eyes and turn on your oven!

triple coconut cookies

MAKES ABOUT 30 COOKIES

Are you a coconut person? Because I'm a coconut person. I would probably put it in everything if given the opportunity. I like to think of these soft and chewy little cookies as bite-sized pieces of vacation. They contain three kinds of coconut: coconut oil, coconut extract, and coconut flakes. It might seem excessive, but I assure you it is not! The oil adds tons of moisture, the extract adds flavor, and the flakes add texture and beauty.

With this recipe, I want you to pay particular attention when you're forming the cookie dough into balls. See if your muscle memory will allow you to pick up precisely the correct amount of dough, by feel (you can test yourself with your kitchen scale!). Notice the dough's smooth, satisfying texture in your hands. Admire the beauty of the sweetened coconut flakes enveloping each ball. Rolling cookie dough often turns into a meditative process for me, where my mind slows down and my shoulders relax. I hope it can do the same for you!

FOR THE COOKIE DOUGH

2½ cups (325g) all-purpose flour

1 teaspoon baking soda

¾ teaspoon kosher salt

1 cup (200g) room temp (not melted) virgin coconut oil

½ cup (100g) dark brown sugar

½ cup (100g) granulated sugar

2 large eggs

½ teaspoon coconut extract

1 teaspoon vanilla extract

1½ cups (168g) sweetened coconut flakes

FOR THE COATING

1 cup (112g) sweetened coconut flakes

the how-to

1   Preheat the oven to 350°F and line a baking sheet with parchment paper.

2   In a medium bowl, whisk together the flour, baking soda, and salt.

3   In the bowl of a stand mixer fitted with the paddle attachment, cream together the coconut oil, brown sugar, and granulated sugar on medium-high speed until creamy, about 3 minutes—scrape down the bowl halfway through to make sure it's mixing evenly. Beat in the eggs on medium speed until thoroughly combined. Add the coconut extract and vanilla extract and beat to combine. Scrape down the bowl. Add the flour mixture all at once and mix on low speed until the dough comes together. Add the coconut flakes and mix on low speed until just combined.

4   Form the dough into 1½-tablespoon (30g) sized balls. Roll each ball in the reserved sweetened coconut flakes covering all of the surfaces. Place the cookies at least 3 inches apart on the baking sheet. Bake for 10 to 11 minutes, until lightly golden around the edges and just set in the middle. Let the cookies cool on the pan for 2 minutes, then transfer them to a wire rack. Store at room temp in an airtight container for up to 3 days.

I'm sorry you're feeling scared right now. Fear can be such an isolating feeling; it can make us believe that we're totally alone in our experience. But please remember: many people care about how you're feeling. Many people are there to listen and support you through whatever it is you're going through.

When I'm scared, I feel a creeping tightness move across my chest and up into my throat. It's sometimes accompanied by a prickling sensation across my cheeks. Can you identify where your fear might be showing up in your body right now? Then, can you close your eyes and imagine a gentle mist flowing to those spots while you breathe in and out through your nose for several breaths?

Now open your eyes and read this:

No matter what happens, you are going to find a way forward. You always have before.

carrot cream cheese bars

MAKES 9 LARGE-ISH BARS

OK, this recipe is a little bit out there, but just a *little*. Imagine if a gooey seven-layer bar had a baby with a cream cheese–frosted carrot cake—sound delicious? Then you'll love these bars. They are **not** cake-like in texture—they've got a layer of shortbread crust, followed by a layer of a rich and sweet cream cheese/carrot mixture that's vaguely cheesecake-like, and finally: crunchy, toasty pecans scattered on the top. Their flavor is bright and fresh, perfect for countering a case of the scaries.

FOR THE SHORTBREAD CRUST

1¼ cups (163g) all-purpose flour
¼ cup (50g) granulated sugar
a pinch of kosher salt
½ cup (1 stick, 113g) melted unsalted butter

FOR THE FILLING

4 oz (113g) room temp cream cheese
¼ cup (50g) granulated sugar
⅔ cup sweetened condensed milk
1 teaspoon vanilla extract
1 teaspoon fresh lemon zest
1 cup (100g) finely chopped (in a food processor) carrots
½ cup (60g) coarsely chopped pecans

ANXIOUS

191

the how-to: shortbread crust

1 Preheat the oven to 350°F. Line the bottom and two sides of an 8-inch square cake pan with an overhanging strip of parchment paper cut to the width of the bottom of the pan. Grease the exposed sides of the pan.

2 In a medium bowl, whisk together the flour, granulated sugar, and salt. Add the melted butter and stir with a rubber spatula until the dough comes together. Add the dough to your prepared pan and, using your fingertips, press it down evenly. Bake the crust for 15 to 17 minutes, until it's lightly golden around the edges. Set aside on a wire rack to cool slightly.

the how-to: filling

1 Meanwhile, in the bowl of a stand mixer fitted with the paddle attachment, beat the cream cheese on medium speed until smooth, about 2 minutes. Add the granulated sugar and beat on medium speed until thoroughly combined, about 2 more minutes. Add the sweetened condensed milk, vanilla extract, and lemon zest and beat on medium speed until incorporated, about 1 minute. Add the carrots and mix on low speed just until combined. Pour the filling over the baked crust. Scatter the pecans over the top.

2 Bake for 30 to 35 minutes, until the edges are lightly golden. Place the bars on a wire rack to cool completely in the pan, then lift them out using the parchment paper sling to slice and serve. Serve room temp or cold from the fridge! Store in the fridge, covered, for up to 3 days.

A lot of times when we feel scattered, we end up shaming ourselves for not being able to "keep it together" in the way that we think other people can. We assume everyone else is able to effortlessly maintain neat and orderly homes, feelings, and lives. But spoiler alert: no one has it all together, and everyone's feelings are complex, messy, and yes—sometimes scattered.

But back to you. Here's a list of things to consider:

- Perhaps your sky-high standards for yourself are not realistic, or fair to you.

- Perhaps you have a lot going on, and a lot on your plate.

- Perhaps you're overextending yourself, although you need and deserve time to rest.

- Perhaps you are human.*

*If you are not, please let me know how you came across this book.

blackberry lime galette

MAKES A 10-INCH GALETTE

I love galettes! They're great for those times when you want something pie-like but you don't have a lot of extra bandwidth. There's no fussy crimping of the crust, no pie plate to unearth. Galettes are messy by design. You roll out the crust, place it on a rimmed baking sheet, plop the filling in, and fold the edges over on top, as is. Believe me, the results will taste just as delicious as a typical pie, without all the hassle.

This simple recipe starts out with my standard pie crust, then it combines two bright and tart ingredients: blackberries and lime. We add sugar for sweetness, and tapioca starch to thicken. By the time it's done baking, the blackberries will have broken down and their juices will be bubbling, lending this galette a deep purple/pink color that is just really aesthetically pleasing.

FOR THE CRUST

1 recipe Single Pie crust (page 238)

FOR THE FILLING

3 cups (435g) blackberries, fresh or frozen
¾ cup (150g) granulated sugar
1 tablespoon fresh lime zest
2 tablespoons fresh lime juice
a pinch of kosher salt
3 tablespoons tapioca starch

1 large egg

1 tablespoon heavy cream

1 tablespoon turbinado sugar

the how-to: crust

1 Preheat the oven to 400°F.

2 Roll out the crust into a 12-inch circle about ⅛ inch thick—it's OK if the edges are not totally even. Transfer it to a parchment paper–lined rimmed baking sheet and pop it in the fridge while you prepare the filling.

the how-to: filling

In a large bowl, stir together the blackberries, granulated sugar, lime zest, lime juice, salt, and tapioca starch. Give it several good stirs to make sure everything's combined evenly.

the how-to: egg wash

In a small bowl, combine the egg and heavy cream.

the how-to: assembly

1 Take the crust out of the fridge and pour the filling into the center (don't leave any juices behind!). Spread the filling out in an even layer, leaving a 1½-inch border around the edge. Fold the crust in and over the filling edge, overlapping and pressing down on the dough to form a tight seal. Using a pastry brush (or your fingers, in a pinch), brush the crust with the egg wash and sprinkle it with the turbinado sugar.

2 Bake for 35 to 40 minutes, until the juices are bubbling and the crust is deeply golden brown. It's OK if some of the juices escape onto the baking sheet—this is a free-form pie, baby!

3 Let the galette cool completely on a wire cooling rack before slicing. Serve with vanilla ice cream. Store at room temp in an airtight container for up to 2 days.

iced pumpkin bread

MAKES A STANDARD LOAF

First, it's important you know that fall is hands-down my favorite season. I love the pumpkin patch and put up my Halloween decor in August— sorry not sorry! But since I live in (very hot) Texas now and you can't have fall year-round anywhere anyway, I have to manufacture that magic, distinctly *fall*, feeling myself. Thankfully, canned pumpkin is available year-round.

Pumpkin bread is a crowd pleaser. And bonus: it's low effort (no stand mixer involved!). My version is spiced with cinnamon, ginger, and nutmeg. I throw in a cup of toasted pecans for both flavor and texture and top it with a glaze to give it a bit of extra shine. It's got a moist, dense crumb —exactly as a pumpkin bread should.

FOR THE PUMPKIN BREAD

½ cup (1 stick, 113g) unsalted butter

2 cups (260g) all-purpose flour

1½ teaspoons baking powder

½ teaspoon baking soda

½ teaspoon kosher salt

1 teaspoon ground cinnamon

¼ teaspoon ground ginger

¼ teaspoon ground nutmeg

1½ cups (336g) canned pumpkin puree

1¼ cups (250g) light brown sugar

3 room temp large eggs

1 tablespoon vanilla extract

1 cup (120g) toasted and coarsely chopped pecans

1 cup (120g) powdered sugar

2 to 3 tablespoons whole milk

1 teaspoon pumpkin puree

¼ teaspoon vanilla extract

the how-to: cake

1   Preheat the oven to 350°F and line the bottom and two sides of a 9 x 5-inch loaf pan with a strip of parchment paper. Grease the pan and parchment paper.

2   Heat a small skillet over medium heat. Add the butter and heat until melted, brown, and nutty, stirring often. Watch it carefully, and remove from the heat as soon as it reaches a deep caramel color. Set aside to cool slightly.

3   In a medium bowl, whisk together the flour, baking powder, baking soda, salt, cinnamon, ginger, and nutmeg.

4   In a large bowl, whisk together the browned butter, pumpkin puree, brown sugar, eggs, and vanilla extract until smooth. Add the dry ingredients to the wet ingredients and stir with a rubber spatula until no streaks of flour remain. Stir in the pecans.

5   Bake for 65 to 70 minutes, until a tester comes out with moist (but not wet!) crumbs. Let cool in the pan for 10 minutes, then turn out onto a wire rack.

the how-to: glaze

In a small bowl, stir together the powdered sugar, milk, pumpkin puree, and vanilla extract. Set a length of wax paper or parchment paper under your cooling rack to catch any drips. Pour the glaze evenly over the still-warm loaf, letting it drip down the sides. Store at room temp in an airtight container for up to a week.

When I'm stressed, I generally don't have the patience to read a wall of text, so I'll get straight to the point! Let's take some time to identify where the stress is showing up in your body with a quick scan. What's your tongue doing? Is your jaw in a vise grip? Are your shoulders up around your ears? Are your hands balled into fists?

Now: take a breath in through your nose, then let it out. Take another. Visualize sending that breath to parts of your body where you notice you're holding on to the stress and tension. Maybe you can send your shoulder blades down your back. Maybe you can unclench your jaw. Our goal here is to try to calm the nervous system and make some space for those feelings that might be simmering underneath the stress. By acknowledging these physical manifestations, you're able to better examine the contours of what's stressing you out, and just as important: comfort your body.

buttermilk pie

MAKES A 9-INCH PIE

We've released some pent-up tension; now let's use our hands! If you've never had a buttermilk pie, you might be thinking, *That sounds kind of gross actually*. I get it. But let me give you some more details. The base is a single very flaky pie crust. Next comes a silky textured filling with a subtle crunch on the top. It has a bold tangy flavor from the lemon and buttermilk, with some extra sweetness from the sliced strawberries scattered decoratively on the surface. It's both beautiful and unique, just like you!

Now's the time to dance it out—Robyn's "Dancing On My Own" is always a great place to start.

FOR THE CRUST

1 recipe Single Pie crust (page 238)

FOR THE FILLING

1 tablespoon fresh lemon zest

1 cup (200g) granulated sugar

3 large eggs

4 tablespoons (½ stick, 57g) melted and
    cooled unsalted butter

¼ cup fresh lemon juice

½ teaspoon vanilla extract

a pinch of kosher salt

¾ cup buttermilk

3 tablespoons all-purpose flour

1 tablespoon fine or medium grind cornmeal

½ cup (84g) strawberries, sliced into ⅛-inch rounds

the how-to: crust

Preheat the oven to 375°F. Prick your pie crust all over with a fork, then freeze it for 30 minutes. Line your pie dish with parchment paper and fill it with pie weights, rice, or dried beans. Place the pie dish on a rimmed baking sheet. Bake for 15 minutes. Remove the parchment paper and pie weights, then bake until the bottom of the crust is lightly golden, 6 to 8 more minutes. Set aside to cool slightly. Reduce the oven temperature to 350°F.

the how-to: filling

1. In a medium bowl, rub the lemon zest into the granulated sugar using your fingertips. Whisk together the lemon-zested sugar and eggs until slightly thickened, about 30 seconds. Add the melted butter, lemon juice, vanilla extract, and salt and whisk until combined. Whisk in the buttermilk. Add the flour and cornmeal and whisk until thoroughly incorporated.

2. Arrange the sliced strawberries in an even layer in the bottom of the pie crust. Pour the buttermilk filling over the strawberries. Bake for 48 to 52 minutes, until just a tiny bit jiggly in the middle. Let cool completely on a wire rack (you can put it in the fridge to hurry this along). Store in the fridge, covered, for up to 2 days.

YOU MIGHT BE FEELING:
*cornered, stuck, like you
aren't sure how to find your
way out of this mess*

For the past several years, I've lived with daily chronic pain. There are days when I just want to go on a vacation and leave my body at home. But, of course, the body and mind are a package deal. Feeling trapped, in your body or otherwise, can be very scary, and I want to take a minute to validate that fear. I've spent a lot of time trying to contort myself into someone who handles her pain. Someone who doesn't inconvenience anyone, doesn't show her suffering, and pushes through. I believed that my inability to maintain a "normal" schedule or keep up the facade that I wasn't struggling indicated some kind of character flaw or weakness. But I wasn't doing myself any favors by trying to minimize my pain, and neither are you.

Maybe the source of your feeling trapped today doesn't have anything to do with your body; maybe you want to leave your thankless, demanding, or simply boring job. Maybe you just want ten minutes to yourself to take a shower without being interrupted. Whatever's got you feeling trapped, take a minute to acknowledge it, but try not to judge yourself. Give yourself a break and make space for how hard things are right now.

white chocolate ginger biscotti

MAKES ABOUT 24 COOKIES

Generally, I'm not a huge biscotti person. I will eat it if someone offers it to me, but it's not like I'm going to seek it out. I think it can be kind of bland, and as you might have noticed, I am of the opinion that chewy cookies almost always beat crunchy. But those opinions shifted when I realized how easy/satisfying it is to make biscotti myself! With biscotti, you need strong flavors to balance out the dry texture. In this recipe, we're taking a macadamia nut–laden biscotti dough base and adding freshly grated ginger, lemon zest, and some white chocolate. It's definitely not boring.

Sometimes you can help manage the feeling of being trapped by trying something new. If you've never made biscotti before (like I hadn't until recently), let's give it a shot.

2 cups + 2 tablespoons (276g) all-purpose flour

1¼ cups (140g) toasted and coarsely chopped
     macadamia nuts

1½ teaspoons baking powder

½ teaspoon kosher salt

1 tablespoon fresh lemon zest

2 teaspoons freshly grated ginger

½ cup (about 70g) chopped white chocolate

½ cup (1 stick, 227g) room temp unsalted butter

½ cup (100g) light brown sugar

¼ cup (50g) granulated sugar

2 large eggs

1 tablespoon vanilla extract

the how-to

1 Preheat the oven to 325°F and line a baking sheet with parchment paper.

2 In a medium bowl, whisk together the flour, macadamia nuts, baking powder, salt, lemon zest, ginger, and chopped white chocolate.

3 In the bowl of a stand mixer fitted with the paddle attachment, cream together the butter, brown sugar, and granulated sugar on medium-high speed until light and fluffy, about 3 minutes. Beat in the eggs and vanilla extract on medium speed until combined. Add the flour mixture and mix on low speed until just combined.

4 Dump the dough out onto a lightly floured surface and divide into two pieces. Roll each piece into a 2-inch log. Place both logs onto your prepared baking sheet and bake for 30 to 35 minutes, until set and golden.

5 Using the parchment paper as a sling, transfer the logs to a rack to cool slightly, about 10 minutes, then transfer to a cutting board. Using a sharp knife, cut the logs at a diagonal into ½-inch-thick slices. Transfer the biscotti back to the baking sheet and bake for another 15 to 18 minutes, flipping over halfway through, until golden. Transfer them back to the cooling rack to cool completely. Store at room temp in an airtight container for up to 2 weeks.

YOU MIGHT BE FEELING:
*nervous, uneasy, a knot
in your stomach or a
furrow in your brow*

Worries run deep, and they can feel like a constant undercurrent to our lives. While you're going about your day, you might also be thinking about what might go wrong with your partner fifteen years from now, or what you need to accomplish next week, or how you're going to handle that tough conversation you've been meaning to have with your friend.

I find that sometimes it helps me get out of my own head to simply grab a pen and write my worries down. That way they're not just jostling around in my head in a loud and repetitive jumble. Sometimes, just seeing those big, scary-seeming worries on paper can make them feel more manageable. And you might find that acknowledging them, rather than trying to push them away, actually diminishes their hold on you.

Remember, you don't have to have everything figured out right now. And it's OK to ask for help when you need it.

swirled pound cake

MAKES A STANDARD LOAF CAKE

I, like, really, really love pound cake. Given the opportunity, I will choose it over many bakery counter items. In fact, I love plain old vanilla pound cake and will often make the simple version instead of fancier options. That said, sometimes you want something a bit more complex, and that's where this cake comes in. We're swirling together thick and rich vanilla batter and chocolate batter and topping it with a crumb topping. If you mess up your swirls a little, no worries—the cake will still be delicious.

FOR THE CRUMB TOPPING

⅓ cup (43g) all-purpose flour
⅓ cup (67g) light brown sugar
a pinch of kosher salt
3 tablespoons (42g) melted unsalted butter

FOR THE CAKE

2 tablespoons Dutch-process cocoa powder
2 tablespoons melted unsalted butter
1¾ cups (228g) all-purpose flour
1½ teaspoons baking powder
½ teaspoon kosher salt
¾ cup (1½ sticks, 170g) room temp unsalted butter
1¼ cups (250g) granulated sugar
3 room temp large eggs
3 room temp large egg yolks
1 tablespoon vanilla extract
⅔ cup (160g) room temp sour cream

the how-to: crumb topping

In a small bowl, stir together all of the crumb topping ingredients using a fork. Set aside.

the how-to: cake

1   Preheat the oven to 350°F and line the bottom and two sides of a 9 x 5-inch loaf pan with a strip of parchment paper. Grease the pan and parchment paper.

2   In a small bowl, stir together the cocoa powder and melted butter until smooth.

3   In a medium bowl, whisk together the flour, baking powder, and salt.

4   In the bowl of a stand mixer, beat the room temp butter on medium-high speed for about 2 minutes, until smooth. Slowly pour in the granulated sugar and beat on medium-high speed for 3 to 4 minutes, until very light and fluffy. Scrape down the sides of the bowl. Add the eggs and egg yolks one at a time (seriously—one at a time!), beating thoroughly, about 30 seconds, on medium speed between each. Scrape down the sides of the bowl. Add the vanilla extract and mix on medium speed until combined. With the mixer running on low, add the flour mixture and sour cream in three alternating batches, until just combined. This will be your vanilla batter.

5   Transfer 1 cup of the vanilla batter to the bowl with the cocoa powder mixture and stir until smooth. This will be your chocolate batter.

6   Spoon half of the vanilla batter into your prepared pan and smooth it evenly using an offset spatula. Spread the chocolate batter on top, then top with the remaining half of the vanilla batter and smooth the top. Swirl the batter with a butter knife (but don't overdo it! Five swirls max!). Gently smooth the top with the offset spatula again. Tap the pan on the counter a couple of times to get rid of any air bubbles.

7   Top with the crumb topping.

8   Bake for 55 to 65 minutes, until a tester comes out with moist (but not wet!) crumbs. Let cool in the pan for 10 minutes, then turn out onto a wire rack to cool completely before slicing. Store at room temp in an airtight container for up to a week.

note: Make sure to separate your egg yolks right out of the fridge! It's much easier to separate cold eggs.

hopeful

The recipes in this chapter are here to match and fuel your excitement.

Vibes: Booking a vacation eight months out, your heart racing when you see *them*, vulnerability—but like in a good way

Ah, hopefulness, that breath of fresh air! This just might be my favorite section of the book. Generally, these feelings are bright, sparkly, and *fun*. If asked, I would say the sensory equivalent is that first scrumptious whiff of freshly bloomed wisteria that gently wafts in through your open window in the springtime.

Maybe you turned to this page because optimism just comes easily to you (incredible!). But I'm not really an optimist by nature, so the feelings in this chapter are ones I actively nurture and cultivate in my life. And I believe that once you start looking for your everyday moments of inspiration, creativity, bravery, etc., you start seeing them everywhere (like when you learn a new word, you start hearing it all the time).

If you're like, *Becca, I'm lost, what do you mean?*—here's a short list of these kinds of everyday expressions of hope I'm talking about:

- Asking that really cute person with the kind eyes out on an ice cream date (this one is from personal experience—it's how I met my husband).

- Buying an assortment of inexpensive flowers and arranging them into several little bouquets (thanks for this one, Sam).

- Going to Ikea/assembling Ikea furniture with someone you love.

- Making a vision board.

- And, of course: trying out a new recipe.

Feelings of hope showcase our beautiful ability to adapt, overcome, and create, despite life's inevitable and many challenges. I'd say that it's one of our most wonderful and helpful qualities as humans. I'm so happy you're here today!

adventurous

brave

confident

creative

curious

inspired

motivated

optimistic

YOU MIGHT BE FEELING:
*bright and shiny, intrepid
in the face of the unknown,
ready to shake things up*

Adventure is such a delicious word. For me, it evokes imagery of blue skies, towering tree-lined mountains, and wide-open spaces with room to make a few mistakes (thanks, The Chicks). I associate it with possibility and exploration. And I've found that simply framing something as an adventure (rather than, say, a task/assignment/chore) is a super motivating way to get yourself moving. My point is that you can feel adventurous about pretty much anything—big and small!

Grappling with a challenge can be exhilarating. And sometimes it just feels good to chase something! But it's especially sweet when the thing you're chasing is adventure. I'm proud of you for bravely going your own way.

glazed donuts

As I mentioned earlier, I *really* love donuts. But I'm going to be honest with you—I'm a cake donut kind of person. If there's a choice, I'm choosing cake. But like once a year I get a craving for that super light sweet fluffiness that only a yeast donut can provide. And that craving is what inspired this recipe.

If you like having options, you'll appreciate that I've provided three glazes here. Choose your own adventure (ha!)—whatever sounds best to you this morning, or afternoon, or evening, or whenever you happen to be whipping these up.

FOR THE DONUTS

1 tablespoon active dry yeast

1½ cups whole milk, warmed to about 95°F

¼ cup (50g) granulated sugar

6 tablespoons (85g) melted and cooled unsalted butter

1 large egg

3 large egg yolks

2 teaspoons vanilla extract

1 teaspoon kosher salt

4¼ cups (552g) all-purpose flour (+ more if your dough feels too wet and for rolling)

lots (like 6 cups!) of vegetable shortening or vegetable oil, for frying

FOR THE LEMON-POPPY SEED GLAZE

2 cups (240g) powdered sugar

1 tablespoon poppy seeds

a pinch of kosher salt

1 teaspoon fresh lemon zest

¼ cup fresh lemon juice

FOR THE VANILLA-COCONUT GLAZE

2 cups (240g) powdered sugar

½ teaspoon vanilla extract

a pinch of kosher salt

¼ cup whole milk

1 cup (112g) sweetened coconut flakes,
    for topping

or

FOR THE HONEY-CINNAMON GLAZE

2 cups (240g) powdered sugar

¼ teaspoon ground cinnamon

½ teaspoon vanilla extract

a pinch of kosher salt

2 tablespoons honey

¼ cup whole milk

the how-to: donuts

1 In a small bowl or glass measuring cup, combine the yeast with the warm milk. Set aside until foamy, about 5 minutes.

2 In the bowl of a stand mixer fitted with the paddle attachment, beat the yeast mixture, sugar, melted butter, egg, egg yolks, vanilla extract, and salt on low speed until combined. Switch to the dough hook. With the mixer running on low, add the flour in three batches. Increase the speed to medium and knead until the dough pulls away from the sides of the bowl, about 5 minutes. The dough will feel sticky, but if it feels *too* sticky, add more flour a tablespoonful at a time.

3 Scrape the dough out onto a floured counter. Wipe out the bowl and lightly coat it with vegetable oil. Transfer the dough back into the bowl, cover with plastic wrap, and let sit out on the counter in a warm spot until doubled in size, 45 minutes to 1 hour depending on how warm your kitchen is.

4 Line two baking sheets with parchment paper and thoroughly flour your countertop. Roll the dough out to ½-inch thickness. Cut out donut shapes about 3 inches wide—you can use a donut cutter, cookie cutter, or the rim of a glass. Use a second 1-inch-wide cutter (or a shot glass!) to make donut holes in the center of each round. Transfer the donuts and donut holes to the prepared baking sheets, at least an inch apart. Cover them with plastic wrap or a kitchen towel and let sit out on the countertop for about 45 minutes—they'll puff up slightly.

the how-to: frying & glaze

1 While the donuts are rising, whisk together your preferred glaze(s). For the vanilla-coconut glaze: whisk together everything except the coconut flakes, then sprinkle them on top after glazing.

2 Line two wire cooling racks with paper towels. About 20 minutes before your donuts are done rising, heat the vegetable oil in a cast-iron skillet or Dutch oven (you'll need a depth of at least 2 inches) with a candy thermometer clipped to the side. When the oil reaches 365°F, you're ready to start frying. Important note: Make sure to wear an apron and stand a safe distance back from the stove in case the

oil splatters a bit! Fry the donuts a few at a time for 1 to 1½ minutes per side (flipping with heatproof tongs), until golden. Drain on a paper towel–lined wire rack. Let cool slightly (but only slightly—the glaze has to go on while the donuts are still hot!).

3   As soon as you can handle them (like 3-ish minutes), dip the warm donuts into the glaze (followed by the sweetened coconut flakes, if you went the vanilla-coconut glaze route). Eat them ASAP. These are best eaten day of.

YOU MIGHT BE FEELING:
*determined, gutsy, ready
to take on the world*

A lot of words come to mind when I think about bravery: *strength, perseverance, self-love.* Being brave can open doors (or windows, or whatever). It's exciting! But usually, being brave is also difficult and messy. Moving outside of what makes you feel comfortable takes work. It requires courage and vulnerability.

I think most people are braver than they give themselves credit for—I'm talking on the daily. It's not just the big stuff like moving to a new city where you don't know anyone. It's speaking up for what you or someone else deserves, changing your mind, or stating a boundary. Cheers to you for wherever your bravery is taking you!

pink lemonade Bundt cake

MAKES A 12-CUP BUNDT CAKE

Are Bundt cakes the cutest cakes? I think so, yes. And this one in particular is really, really cute (pink icing!). It's the perfect reward for being brave—no matter how big or small the feat. It's up for debate what flavor pink lemonade actually is—strawberry? raspberry? cherry? But for this recipe, I've decided the pink stands for raspberry. This is a tart and refreshing lemon cake with swirls of sweet raspberry jam throughout. Since it's baked in a Bundt pan, it's perfect for feeding a lot of people at once. It also keeps very well. In other words, it's holiday ready (pretty much any holiday).

I paired this recipe with "brave" because Bundt cakes can be intimidating. The key is to grease the pan *extremely* well—you can use your fingers, but a pastry brush works especially well. Every nook and cranny of the pan needs to be coated to make sure that your cake will slide right out, perfectly intact.

FOR THE CAKE

3 cups (390g) all-purpose flour

½ teaspoon baking powder

½ teaspoon baking soda

1 teaspoon kosher salt

¾ cup buttermilk

⅓ cup fresh lemon juice

1 tablespoon vanilla extract

⅓ cup (40g) loosely packed fresh lemon zest

2 cups (400g) granulated sugar

1 cup (2 sticks, 227g) room temp unsalted butter

5 room temp large eggs

½ cup (150g) seedless raspberry preserves

FOR THE ICING

2 cups (240g) powdered sugar

3 to 4 tablespoons fresh lemon juice

1 tablespoon seedless raspberry preserves

¼ teaspoon vanilla extract

the how-to: cake

1   Preheat the oven to 350°F. Coat a 12-cup Bundt pan with softened butter—make sure to coat every single nook and cranny. Sprinkle flour evenly over the pan, then tap out the excess.

2   In a medium bowl, whisk together the flour, baking powder, baking soda, and salt.

3   In a glass measuring cup or small bowl, stir together the buttermilk, lemon juice, and vanilla extract.

4   In the bowl of a stand mixer fitted with the paddle attachment, rub the lemon zest into the granulated sugar using your fingertips (this will give us a lot more flavor!). Add the butter and beat on medium-high speed for about 4 minutes, until very light and fluffy. Scrape down the sides of the bowl. Add the eggs one at a time (seriously—one at a time!), beating thoroughly, about 30 seconds, on medium speed between each. Scrape down the sides of the bowl. With the mixer running on low, add the flour and buttermilk mixture in three alternating batches, until just combined.

5   Add half of the batter to the Bundt pan. Add half of the raspberry preserves, dropping by the spoonful around the pan in a random (but roughly evenly spaced) pattern. Swirl the preserves into the batter with a butter knife. Add the second half of the batter, then repeat your raspberry swirls. Smooth the top and tap the pan on the counter a couple of times to remove air bubbles.

6   Bake for 45 to 50 minutes, until the top of the cake is golden and a tester inserted comes out with moist crumbs. Let cool for 10 minutes in the pan, then turn it out onto a wire rack to cool completely before icing. When you flip it over, leave the pan on top of the cake for 30 seconds before lifting it off—it should drop right out!

the how-to: icing

In a small bowl, stir together the powdered sugar, lemon juice, raspberry preserves, and vanilla extract. Since we want those pretty drips that stop halfway down the cake, we're looking for a thick icing here. Set a length of wax paper or parchment paper under your cooling rack to catch any drips. Spoon the icing over the completely cooled cake evenly, letting it run down the sides. Store in an airtight container out on the counter for up to 5 days.

note: If you don't have a Bundt pan, try making this recipe in two 9 x 5-inch loaf pans! The bake time might be 5 minutes longer—just keep checking for doneness.

CONFIDENT

~~~~~~

YOU MIGHT BE FEELING:
*self-assured, unfazed, like
you've got your shit together and
everything's going to be fine*

~~~~~~

Yay for believing in yourself! Do you feel that inner glow? Because I can almost feel it radiating through the pages of this book. It's so wonderful that at this very moment you're trusting yourself and your instincts, expertise, and wisdom (and rightfully so!).

It takes a lot of work to counter the pesky false narrative you might have been fed that says something along the lines of "you just aren't the right person for the job." It's so common to feel like you're some kind of imposter, but I'm here to confirm that it's not true. Congratulations for banishing that unhelpful thought (even if it's just for now!).

You've got this, I just know it.

banana layer cake

MAKES AN 8-INCH 3-LAYER CAKE

I first made this cake for my former neighbor Audrey's third birthday party. She requested a banana cake, and though I had never made one before, I gave it a shot. Turns out her vision was spot-on—the scraps I tried were delicious. I brought the triple-layered monstrosity over to her house the night before the party, came over the next day, and noticed that a very noticeable three-year-old-hand-shaped swipe had been taken out of the side! It made me quite proud, because I truly believe you should eat your birthday cake whenever you want. And the sheer confidence in grabbing a little pre-party snack for herself, without fear of repercussion, is inspiring.

FOR THE CAKE

3½ cups (455g) all-purpose flour

2 cups (400g) light brown sugar

½ cup (100g) granulated sugar

2½ teaspoons baking powder

½ teaspoon baking soda

1 teaspoon ground cinnamon

1 teaspoon kosher salt

1½ cups (from about 4) very ripe mashed bananas

½ cup (120g) room temp sour cream

¾ cup vegetable oil

3 room temp large eggs

1 tablespoon vanilla extract

1½ cups (3 sticks, 345g) room temp unsalted butter

6 cups (720g) powdered sugar

1 teaspoon ground cinnamon

3 to 4 tablespoons heavy cream

2 teaspoons vanilla extract

the how-to: cake

1 Preheat the oven to 350°F. Line three 8-inch round cake pans with parchment paper. Grease the pans with softened butter.

2 In a large bowl, whisk together the flour, brown sugar, granulated sugar, baking powder, baking soda, cinnamon, and salt. In another large bowl, whisk together the mashed banana, sour cream, vegetable oil, eggs, and vanilla extract until smooth.

3 Pour the wet ingredients into the dry ingredients. Mix with a rubber spatula until there are no visible streaks of flour.

4 Scrape the batter into the prepared pans. Bake for 30 to 34 minutes, until deeply golden and a tester comes out clean. Cool for 10 minutes in the pan, then turn layers out onto a wire rack to cool completely.

the how-to: cinnamon buttercream & assembly

1 In the bowl of a stand mixer fitted with the paddle attachment, beat the butter on medium-high speed until light and fluffy, about 3 minutes. Slowly beat in the powdered sugar on medium speed. Continue beating for 2 minutes. Add the cinnamon, heavy cream, and vanilla extract and beat until combined.

2 Level the cakes, fill, and frost. Store at room temp in an airtight container for up to 3 days.

Being creative doesn't just mean making pottery. I mean it *can* obviously, but creativity comes in so many forms. Maybe you came up with a new way to tactfully navigate a difficult conversation. Maybe you rearranged your living room to optimize the afternoon sunlight for your cat. Maybe you invented a new sandwich and it's like *so* amazing. Embracing creativity means suspending your judgments of yourself. It means giving yourself permission to be playful.

And it feels so expansive! Perhaps you're feeling like pushing out boundaries, shedding some conventions, or forging a new path. Perhaps you're just making something in your daily life more interesting. Yay for whatever it is!

And if you're feeling the creative juices flowing today but aren't sure where to direct them, let me suggest making this free-form galette with cherries on top.

almond cherry galette

MAKES A 10-INCH GALETTE

This recipe comes from merging two of my all-time favorite flavors. First: I love the tart sweetness of cherries, not to mention their beautiful deep red color. And second: I *really* love almond frangipane. It reminds me of these truly incredible S-shaped pastries I would get as a child from an Amish bakery in Missouri (if you're interested, I think they're typically called Dutch letters). So, with this recipe we're getting creative by combining the two flavors and pairing them with my flaky all-butter pie crust. The first time I made and tasted this, I actually said "oh my god" out loud. Who knew innovation could taste so good.

FOR THE CRUST

1 recipe Single Pie crust (page 238)

FOR THE ALMOND FILLING

½ cup (70g) blanched slivered almonds

⅓ cup (67g) granulated sugar

1 large egg

4 tablespoons (½ stick, 57g) room temp unsalted butter

1 tablespoon all-purpose flour

a pinch of kosher salt

¾ teaspoon vanilla extract

¼ teaspoon almond extract

2 cups (226g) frozen sweet cherries

FOR THE EGG WASH

1 large egg
1 tablespoon heavy cream

FOR THE TOPPING

1 tablespoon granulated sugar

the how-to: almond filling

1 Preheat the oven to 400°F.

2 Place the almonds and granulated sugar in the work bowl of a food processor and process until finely ground. Add the egg and run the food processor until combined. Add the butter, flour, salt, vanilla extract, and almond extract and process until smooth. Set aside until needed (it will thicken up just a bit).

the how-to: crust

Roll out the crust into a 12-inch circle about ⅛ inch thick—it's OK if the edges are not totally even. Transfer it to a parchment paper–lined rimmed baking sheet.

the how-to: egg wash

In a small bowl, combine the egg and heavy cream.

the how-to: assembly

1 Pour the almond filling into the center of the crust. Gently spread it out in an even layer, leaving a 1½-inch border around the edge. Scatter the cherries evenly over the top. Fold the crust in and over the filling edge, overlapping and pinching the dough together to form a tight seal. Using a pastry brush (or your fingers, in a pinch), brush the crust with the egg wash. Sprinkle the 1 tablespoon of granulated sugar over the cherries.

2 Bake for 35 to 38 minutes, until the almond cream is puffed up and the crust is deeply golden brown. Let the galette cool completely on a wire cooling rack before slicing. Store in the fridge, covered, for up to 3 days.

When I'm feeling curious, I like to channel my eight-year-old self. She spent a lot of time checking out library books about mummification in ancient Egypt, asking garden-related questions like *How do you know when to harvest a watermelon?*, and inventing new methods for painting landscapes with sidewalk chalk. She was uninhibited in her curiosity. I bet your eight-year-old self was too! So: How about channeling eight-year-old you and check out a book/ watch a documentary/etc. on a subject you know nothing about?

Curiosity showcases our passions and expands our bubble. It allows us to feel like we're truly existing in the world, in a refreshing and genuine way. It feels like getting your hands dirty. Speaking of: let's make thumbprints.

peach jam thumbprints

MAKES ABOUT 28 COOKIES

When you're a small child, you bravely explore the world tactilely—using your hands and mouth to investigate texture. Let's revisit this mode of experience in the kitchen! I love the taste of these cookies, but I also really enjoy making thumbprints because the process is so enjoyable. I love pinching off a section of the smooth dough and rolling it in my palms into evenly sized balls. I love noticing the particular shape of the indentation that only my own thumb makes. After all, there are few things more satisfying than mashing your thumb into freshly made cookie dough.

These cookies have a warm and nutty flavor from the toasted pecans, paired with the bright summeriness of peach jam. They're a twist on a classic, which is hard to beat.

FOR THE COOKIES

1 cup (120g) toasted pecans
1¼ cups (163g) all-purpose flour
¾ cup (1½ sticks, 170g) room temp unsalted butter
⅔ cup (133g) light brown sugar
2 large egg yolks
1½ teaspoons vanilla extract

FOR THE FILLING

½ cup (160g) peach jam

the how-to: cookies

1 Pulse the pecans and flour in a food processor until the nuts are very finely ground.

2 In the bowl of a stand mixer fitted with the paddle attachment, beat the butter and brown sugar on medium-high speed until smooth and creamy, about 2 minutes. Add the egg yolks and vanilla extract and mix on medium speed until thoroughly incorporated. Add the dry ingredients and mix on low speed just until the dough comes together. Cover and chill the dough for 1 hour.

the how-to: assembly

1 Preheat the oven to 350°F and line a baking sheet with parchment paper.

2 Scoop the dough into 1-tablespoon (20g) sized balls and arrange them at least 2 inches apart on your baking sheet. Using your thumb, make a deep indentation in the center of each ball. Place ½ teaspoon of jam in each indentation.

3 Bake for 12 to 14 minutes, until the cookies are golden around the edges. Store at room temp in an airtight container for up to 5 days.

~~~~~~

YOU MIGHT BE FEELING:
uplifted, excited, overwhelmed
by the sheer possibility of it all

~~~~~~

This is such a vibey one. To me, inspiration is all about connection. That could mean connecting with a person, a place, or maybe something like a work of art. Maybe you're feeling moved to take action. Maybe you're feeling a deep admiration or appreciation for another human. Whatever it is, how exciting.

Sometimes inspiration comes in the form of a sudden "aha!"/lightbulb moment. That's how the idea of this book came about. I was sitting on my couch one evening and was like, "You know what would be cool? A book where you can figure out your feelings through baking." I stream-of-consciousness-style wrote my ideas until I ran out of them, and then straightened it out into a cohesive "thing" later on. I'm still not quite sure how it popped into my head. But inspiration can also be more of a long-game thing, like a puzzle you put together over time. Either way, great job nurturing your spark.

blueberry cornmeal muffins

MAKES 12 MUFFINS

These breakfast treats are *inspired* by my favorite (sweet/savory, incredibly moist, crunchy-lidded) muffins at my favorite bakery in DC, Elle. They've got cornmeal in them, but they definitely aren't like the cornbread you eat with chili. Filled with juicy blueberries, they're basically summertime in a breakfast pastry. I like to put one in a bowl, pour milk over the top, and dig in with a spoon (just trust me!).

FOR THE MUFFINS

2 cups (260g) all-purpose flour

½ cup (80g) coarsely ground cornmeal

¾ cup (150g) granulated sugar

¼ cup (50g) light brown sugar

1 tablespoon baking powder

1 teaspoon kosher salt

¼ teaspoon ground nutmeg

1 cup (140g) blueberries (I usually use frozen, but fresh work too)

1½ cups (360g) sour cream

½ cup (1 stick, 113g) melted unsalted butter

2 large eggs

2 large egg yolks

1 tablespoon vanilla extract

FOR THE TOPPING

¼ cup (35g) blueberries

2 tablespoons turbinado sugar

the how-to

1. Preheat the oven to 425°F and grease a 12-cup muffin tin with butter (make sure you grease around the tops of the cups too!).

2. In a large bowl, whisk together the flour, cornmeal, granulated sugar, light brown sugar, baking powder, salt, and nutmeg. Stir in the 1 cup blueberries.

3. In a medium bowl, whisk together the sour cream, melted butter, eggs, egg yolks, and vanilla extract. Add the wet ingredients to the dry ingredients and mix just until combined.

4. Spoon the batter evenly into each muffin well—it will reach all the way to the top. Top with the ¼ cup blueberries (about 4 blueberries per muffin) and turbinado sugar.

5. Bake for 24 to 27 minutes, until a tester inserted in the center of a muffin comes out with moist crumbs. Let the muffins cool for 5 minutes in the pan, then transfer to a wire cooling rack to cool completely. Store at room temp in an airtight container for up to 3 days.

MOTIVATED

YOU MIGHT BE FEELING:
*energized, brimming with
passion, like you're finally ready
to cross that one obnoxious
lingering task off your to-do list*

OK, so: this was actually one of the more difficult feelings for me to write about. In fact, it was among the very last ones I wrote—maybe a week before I had to turn my manuscript in. I kept coming back to it, struggling to find something *motivating* to say. So I'm going to be honest here: a lot of the time, motivation feels pretty elusive to me. Sometimes it seems like the harder I chase it, the further away it drifts. Access to feelings of motivation can easily get tangled up in feelings of anxiety and doubt. It can feel really frustrating.

So let me tell you: it doesn't matter whether your feeling of motivation today comes from pure creative inspiration or dedicated self-discipline. The point is, you're doing it. You're exemplifying a beautiful belief in life's possibilities. So get out there and get that thing started (whatever that thing is!). I admire you so much.

oat pie

MAKES A 9-INCH PIE

This recipe reminds me of a very yummy cookie they sometimes served in the lunchroom at my elementary school. And speaking of elementary school: my second- to fifth-grade self was *highly* motivated. For instance, I used to take detailed notes on the videos we watched (about frogs, space, Eleanor Roosevelt, etc.) and turn them in afterward to my (very patient) teacher. Note: This was very much not required, and I'm fairly certain I was the only ten-year-old in the class who assigned themselves extra work. I was just so excited to learn! When I think about it now, I'm kind of in awe of my tiny self. I can't quite relate to that impulse anymore, but sometimes I try to channel it when I'm struggling with self-motivation.

It definitely takes some motivation to make pie, so let's take advantage of today's energy to bake one! I'm not sure if this is a Midwestern thing, but I really love oat pies. And I *especially* love them when they taste like butterscotch and contain cinnamon and chocolate chips. This pie has a super-satisfying gooey, sticky texture—think seven-layer bars but with the bonus of a flaky pie crust base.

FOR THE CRUST

1 recipe Single Pie crust (page 238)

FOR THE FILLING

6 tablespoons (85g) unsalted butter
1½ cups (300g) dark brown sugar

¾ cup heavy cream

2 teaspoons vanilla extract

½ teaspoon kosher salt

½ teaspoon ground cinnamon

3 large eggs

1¼ cups (125g) old-fashioned rolled oats

½ cup (88g) semisweet chocolate chips

the how-to: crust

1   Preheat the oven to 350°F and pull out a 9-inch pie plate.

2   Roll out your pie crust into an 11-inch circle, place it in the pie plate, fold the edges over, and decoratively crimp them. Place the pie crust in the freezer to chill while you prepare the filling.

the how-to: filling

1   In a medium skillet over medium heat, melt the butter. Add the brown sugar and heavy cream and stir with a rubber spatula until combined. Bring the mixture to a simmer and cook for 3 minutes, stirring occasionally. Remove the mixture from the heat and scrape it into a heatproof medium bowl. Stir in the vanilla extract, salt, and cinnamon. Let it cool out on the counter for about 10 minutes. Whisk in the eggs, one at a time, then stir in the rolled oats.

2   Pour the mixture into your prepared pie crust. Top evenly with the chocolate chips. Bake for 45 to 50 minutes, until set. Let cool completely on a wire rack, then serve with vanilla ice cream! Store in the fridge, covered, for up to 3 days.

OPTIMISTIC

YOU MIGHT BE FEELING:
*encouraged, buoyant, pretty
sure that it's going to work out!*

I grew up believing pessimism took up a much bigger slice of my existence than it did. For some reason, there's this engrained social thing where we're told that either a: we're an optimistic person, or b: we're a pessimistic person. The logic behind this binary thinking goes something like: if you outwardly exhibit optimism, you must also be a happy and caring person—if you don't, you're probably an unhappy and uncaring one. As if it's a litmus test for goodness! It's not, of course. Optimism doesn't have to be your defining characteristic. You are allowed to feel and exhibit optimism, regardless of whether you identify as an "optimist" or not. Your optimism shines through when you make a new friend and when you get up after falling down (metaphorically speaking, and literally). It's OK to recognize and celebrate those forms of optimism too.

If I had to come up with an analogous natural phenomenon for feeling optimistic, I'd say it's like those new blooms that peek out after a rainstorm in March despite cold, unwelcoming temperatures. Optimism inherently has some bravery mixed in. It takes courage to trust that things are going to turn out like they should!

cardamom caramel poke cake

MAKES AN 8-INCH SQUARE SINGLE-LAYER CAKE

Hey, I heard you're feeling optimistic! So, today let's tackle a brand-new recipe with a technique you may not have tried before. It might seem counterintuitive, but we're going to poke a bunch of holes in our beautiful freshly baked cake and then fill them with something delicious. Feel free to freestyle it—there's no need to make these holes perfectly spaced or exactly the same depth. It will taste delicious regardless.

Typically poke cakes are filled with something like Jell-O or pudding. But in this version, we're pourin' in some gooey cardamom-infused caramel. It's an elevated basic if I've ever seen one.

FOR THE CAKE

1½ cups (195g) cake flour
1½ teaspoons baking powder
¼ teaspoon kosher salt
½ cup (1 stick, 113g) unsalted butter
¾ cup (150g) granulated sugar
3 large egg whites
2 teaspoons vanilla extract
½ cup whole milk

FOR THE CARAMEL

½ cup (100g) granulated sugar
2 tablespoons water
¼ cup heavy cream
1½ teaspoons unsalted butter
¼ teaspoon vanilla extract
¼ teaspoon ground cardamom

1 cup heavy cream

2 tablespoons powdered sugar

½ teaspoon vanilla extract

the how-to: cake

1 Preheat the oven to 350°F. Line the bottom and two sides of an 8-inch square cake pan with an overhanging strip of parchment paper cut to the width of the bottom of the pan. Grease the exposed sides of the pan and parchment paper.

2 In a medium bowl, whisk together the cake flour, baking powder, and salt.

3 In the bowl of a stand mixer fitted with the paddle attachment, cream together the butter and granulated sugar on medium-high speed until smooth, about 2 minutes. Add the egg whites one at a time, beating until thoroughly incorporated. Add the vanilla extract. With the mixer running on low, add the flour mixture and milk in two alternating batches. Mix just until combined.

4 Pour the batter into your prepared pan. Bake for 28 to 30 minutes, until the edges of the cake are golden. As soon as the cake comes out of the oven, poke holes! Using a tool like a thin-handled wooden spoon, a thick-ish chopstick, or (in a pinch!) a butter knife, poke holes all over the warm cake, about ½ inch apart and about halfway deep. Note: leave the cake in the pan—you'll serve directly out of it.

the how-to: caramel

1 While the cake is in the oven, combine the granulated sugar and water in a medium heavy-bottomed pot. Cook the mixture over medium heat until the sugar dissolves. Just hang tight and don't stir—if you do, it will get clumpy. When the mixture turns a deep golden color, you can start stirring. Stir until smooth. Remove it from the heat and whisk in the heavy cream, butter, vanilla, and cardamom.

2 Pour the caramel into a small heatproof bowl and set aside until needed

3 As soon as you've poked the holes in your cake, pour the caramel evenly over the cake, aiming for the holes, but no worries if it gets all over the top. Set aside to cool completely in the pan.

the how-to: whipped cream

1 Once the cake is completely cool, start the whipped cream. In the bowl of a stand mixer fitted with the whisk attachment, beat the heavy cream, powdered sugar, and vanilla extract on medium-high speed until soft peaks form, about 3 minutes.

2 Plop the whipped cream on top of the cake and spread it out into an even layer. Serve! Store in the fridge, covered, for up to 2 days (but whipped cream will have the best texture day of!).

note: I know it's tempting, but don't use your fingers to poke the holes in the cake! You will burn yourself!

pie crust

I love pie crust. And more specifically: I love *flaky* pie crust. This recipe makes a very flaky, all-butter crust that works with both sweet and savory fillings.

I enjoy everything about pie crust: rolling it, shaping it, cutting it, crimping it. I love assembling my ingredients: a snow shower of flour, sparkly sugar, very *very* cold butter, water, and cream. I love the simple satisfaction when it comes together into a cohesive pastry with just the right consistency: not too dry, not too wet, and perfectly butter-flecked. And I love that first bite, when the crust shatters into golden flakes that somehow always end up all over your face. Because of its tactile, involved, and satisfying process, working with pie crust is a great way to process a variety of feelings. I find it works particularly well for days when you're looking to (or *should* be looking to!) slow down and sit with the feeling.

FOR A SINGLE PIE CRUST	FOR A DOUBLE PIE CRUST
½ cup (1 stick, 113g) cold unsalted butter	1 cup (2 sticks, 226g) cold unsalted butter
3 tablespoons ice water	6 tablespoons ice water
1 cup (130g) all-purpose flour	2 cups (260g) all-purpose flour
1 tablespoon granulated sugar	2 tablespoons granulated sugar
½ teaspoon kosher salt	1 teaspoon kosher salt
1 tablespoon cold heavy cream	2 tablespoons cold heavy cream

the how-to:
Cut your butter into ½-inch chunks. Place the butter chunks on a plate and pop the plate in the freezer to chill out for 5 minutes. Add some ice cubes and about ½ cup of water to a liquid measuring cup. In a medium bowl, whisk together the flour, granulated sugar, and salt. Using your fingertips, work the butter chunks into the flour mixture until sandy. But don't overdo it! The largest pieces should be the size of black beans. Pour in the heavy cream and 3 tablespoons of ice water (or 6, if you're making a double crust). Stir with a rubber spatula, then knead with your hands until it holds together. If the dough feels too dry, you can add some more ice water, a tablespoonful at a time, until it comes together.

for a single crust:
Flatten the dough into a disk and wrap in plastic wrap. Refrigerate for at least an hour or freeze for at least half an hour before using. You can store the prepared dough for up to two days in the fridge, or up to three months in the freezer.

for a double crust:

Divide the dough into two sections. Flatten each section into a disk and wrap in plastic wrap. Refrigerate for at least an hour or freeze for at least half an hour before using. You can store the prepared dough for up to two days in the fridge, or up to three months in the freezer.

inspirations & acknowledgments

This book grew out of my love for a good yellow cake recipe. But it also grew out of my (ongoing!) experiences with anxiety and depression, and the life-giving therapy that has helped me make sense of my own feelings. I wrote it with an immeasurable amount of thanks to my own therapist, Emily, as well as to Sam and Adriana, who are each *someone's* therapist but to me are just extremely emotionally supportive friends. Other non-therapist sources of support for feeling my feelings and writing this book include my sister, Isabel; my brother, Sam; my mom, Melinda; my chosen family members Aarti and Anna; my biggest fans Lizzie and Meg; my in-laws, Alicia and Rudy; my husband, Rhys; and all of the Sweet Feminists out there.

A huge thank-you to the people who brought *Baking by Feel* to life: Jenni Ferrari-Adler, Julie Will, Emma Kupor, Leah Carlson-Stanisic, Amy Scott, and Olivia Caminiti. I immensely appreciate your expertise, creativity, and support.

Thank you to the Curable app.

Thank you to *Foods with Moods: A First Book of Feelings*, by Joost Elfers and Saxton Freymann.

And lastly, an incomplete list of the many bakers and makers who inspire me—I've learned so much from their books, blogs, and bakeries.

Dorie Greenspan
Molly Yeh
Sarah Kieffer
Deb Perelman
Maya-Camille Broussard
Cheryl Day
Samin Nosrat
Lauren Ko
Tangerine Jones
Odette Williams
Arley Arrington
Allie Smith
Teresa Velazquez
Jocelyn Delk Adams
Erin Jeanne McDowell
Danielle Muench
Jane Rea
Christina Tosi
Paola Velez
Jennifer Perillo
Ismael Neggaz
Ruth Wakefield
Michelle Lopez
Jonny Uribe
Yuri Oberbillig

index

about the author

Becca Rea-Tucker's first foray into baking came in the form of licking the cookie dough off the beaters while watching her grandma make chocolate chip cookies. She is a baker, recipe-writer, feelings-haver, and the strong-willed voice behind the oft-shared Instagram account @thesweetfeminist. She lives in Austin, Texas, with her husband, Rhys, and pup, Otis.